The
Martin Buber–Carl Rogers
Dialogue

Martin Buber

Carl Rogers

SUNY Series in Speech Communication
Edited by Dudley D. Cahn, Jr.

The
Martin Buber–Carl Rogers
Dialogue

A New Transcript with Commentary

Rob Anderson
and
Kenneth N. Cissna

STATE UNIVERSITY OF NEW YORK PRESS

Published by
State University of New York Press, Albany

©1997 Rob Anderson and Kenneth N. Cissna

The photograph of Martin Buber was provided by his granddaughter, Judith Buber Agassi, and is reproduced with her permission. Photo credit: M. Huttman. The Carl Rogers photograph was provided by his daughter, Natalie Rogers, and is used with her permission. Photo credit: Louise Barker.

Printed in the United States of America

For information, address State University of New York Press, State University Plaza, Albany, N.Y. 12246

Production by Cathleen Collins
Marketing by Dana Yanulavich

Library of Congress Cataloging in Publication Data

Buber, Martin, 1878–1965.
    The Martin Buber–Carl Rogers dialogue : a new transcript with commentary / Rob Anderson and Kenneth N. Cissna.
       p. cm. — (SUNY series in speech communication)
    Includes bibliographical references and index.
    ISBN 0-7914-3437-0 (alk. paper). — ISBN 0-7914-3438-9 (pbk. : alk. paper)
    1. Dialogue.   2. Interpersonal communication.   3. Philosophical anthropology.   I. Rogers, Carl R. (Carl Ransom), 1902–1987.
II. Anderson, Rob, 1945– .   III. Cissna, Kenneth N. IV. Title.
V. Series.
B3213.B83M37 1997
150′.92′2—dc20
                                        96-44106
                                             CIP

10 9 8 7 6 5 4 3 2 1

To Dona and Susan,
our favorite partners in dialogue

Contents

Preface

Recently, one of us presented a brief informal talk about contemporary research into dialogue in the human sciences. In a small audience of teachers and students, two colleagues reacted in especially intriguing ways. Both are intelligent, friendly, humane, and highly committed to enhancing human interaction. One came from a background in literary criticism, the other from quantitative social science. Citing different reasons, each expressed a similar strong skepticism: Dialogue, although a worthy goal, is impossible given the nature of human cultural experience and today's complex media environment.

Such skepticism (and, beyond it, a more disturbing creeping social cynicism) is common, yet by itself skepticism will not demonstrate that studying dialogue is impractical. It only reminds researchers that they should assume the responsibility to study dialogue and its potential in the most realistic, the most concrete, and the most pragmatic ways possible. Such fields as cultural studies, sociology, anthropology, communication, and psychology are increasingly interested in pluralistic dialogue, and philosophers, of course, have continued to explore its essence. What would be most helpful now, however, are studies of how the philosophical and the practical aspects of dialogic interaction can be blended.

In this monograph, we argue that one especially realistic approach to dialogue is to focus on an actual historical meeting at the intellectual junction of the *philosophical* and the *practical*. Accordingly, for several years we have placed a single communication event at the symbolic center of our dialogue project: The 1957 meeting of philosopher Martin Buber and psychologist Carl Rogers at a University of Michigan conference celebrating Buber's thought. This hour and a half conversation, conducted on stage and taped, brought face-to-face Martin Buber, to one biographer "the most radical religious thinker of his age" and "the most influential religious thinker of the twentieth century" (Streiker, 1969, p. 12) with Carl Rogers, to his biographer the "most influential psychotherapist" and "one of the most influential psychologists" in American history (Kirschenbaum, 1995, p. 98). While Buber emphasized an eloquent delineation of human dialogue, Rogers—from his experience with thousands of clients—had charted some of its praxis. Therefore, the Buber-Rogers dialogue, because it explicitly focused on the nature of dialogue, formed perhaps our richest available touchstone text for examining the philosophical in light of the practical, and the practical dimensions of dialogue in their conceptual context.

Unfortunately, we have discovered that all available published transcripts of this touchstone text are flawed and inaccurate, in hundreds of ways, large and small. After locating a reliable copy of the audiotape made that evening, we set out to clarify the historical record. This brief book, therefore, corrects the earlier errors by presenting a new transcript, discusses the significance of the transcriptional errors and corrections, and examines the implications of the Buber-Rogers interchange for understanding dialogic thought more generally. We want to note that no transcript of this encounter, including ours, could ever be unimprovable. Although our transcript is *much* better than existing transcripts, given the age and ambiguous audibility of the tape it is possible that someone else who listened to the tape could improve on our work. In fact, careful readers of our work may note some minor refinements to our own previously published quotations from the dialogue.

We intend this volume as a disciplined exercise in intellectual history. Buber and Rogers explored crucial topics that we must consider in order to understand the multicultural challenges of a rapidly approaching new century.

Acknowledgments

We acknowledge, first, those who helped us secure copies of the audiotape of the Buber-Rogers dialogue. The first tape we obtained was provided by John Stewart of the University of Washington, to whom we were referred by Maurice Friedman, the dialogue's moderator, who had sent a copy to Professor Stewart. Most of our work on the dialogue was based on this tape. Later Barbara T. Brodley sent us a copy of the partial tape that is in the possession of the Chicago Counseling and Psychotherapy Center. DeWitt C. Baldwin, Jr., told us about donating his father's copy of the tape to the University of California at Santa Barbara, and David E. Russell, Director of the Oral History Program and Humanistic Psychology Archive at UCSB, kindly provided us with a fine copy of what was the best and most complete tape that we were able to obtain.

Professor Emeritus Maurice Friedman of San Diego State University graciously encouraged us in pursuing this project, even as he disagreed with us about several matters. His is a model of open scholarship we respect enormously. He answered our questions about Buber, Rogers, and the event, and generously allowed us access to relevant letters from the 1950s that he exchanged with Martin Buber. Despite our considerable debt to Professor Friedman, readers should not assume that he either sanctions this particular transcript or agrees with all of our interpretations.

Research grants from the Graduate Schools at our institutions were quite helpful along the way. In addition, several graduate students at Saint Louis University also assisted us in our research; we are grateful to Kevin O'Leary, Thao Dang, Michael Williams, and especially Mary Cox. We have played portions of the tape to several undergraduate and graduate seminars and two colloquia, and we appreciate the responses of those groups.

We also thank Dominik Biemann, Martha Mathis, and the staffs of the Martin Buber Archives at the Jewish National & University Library;

xii	*Acknowledgments*

the Michigan Historical Collection at the Bentley Historical Library and the Harlan Hatcher Graduate Library, both of the University of Michigan; the Carl R. Rogers Collection at the Library of Congress; and the Carl Rogers Memorial Library at the Center for Studies of the Person—all of whom helped us obtain documents that have illuminated aspects of the event for us.

Many other people also helped us in this project—by sharing their recollections of the event or of the principals, or by guiding us to other people and resources. In this regard, we thank Judith Buber Agassi, C. Grey Austin, DeWitt C. Baldwin, Jr., Dorothy Becker, Russell J. Becker, Seymour Cain, Charlotte Ellinwood, Richard Farson, Eugene Gendlin, Robert Hauert, Nel Kandel, Howard Kirschenbaum, Robert Lipgar, Betty Lou Mahone, Charles Mahone, William McKeachie, Louis Orlin, Natalie Rogers, John M. Shlien, Len Scott, as well as Tom Greening, who edits the *Journal of Humanistic Psychology* and published our first essay on the dialogue. Only after our article was published did we learn that he was present for the dialogue. When we asked him about it, his answer could apply to life itself. He said that he was an overworked graduate student at the time and didn't remember very much (who could?—it was more than 30 years earlier), and he added: "If I had known it was going to be so important, I would have paid more attention."

Cooperation and coauthorship in our ongoing dialogue investigation has been so multileveled and thorough that we no longer try to keep track of who is the "lead" author of each manuscript. Instead, we have adopted the common convention of alternating the order of our names from project to project.

Introduction

Attending Faithfully to Word, Texture, and Connection

Let us assume I am discussing a text from our literature. It has been interpreted countless times and in
countless ways. I know that no interpretation, including my own, coincides with the original meaning of the
text. I know that my interpreting, like everyone else's,
is conditioned through my being. But if I attend as
faithfully as I can to what it contains of word and tex-
ture, of sound and rhythmic structure, of open and hidden connections, my interpretation will not have been
made in vain—I find something, I have found something. And if I show what I have found, I guide him
who lets himself be guided to the reality of the text. To
him whom I teach I make visible the working forces of
the text that I have experienced.
—Martin Buber, *Pointing the Way*

Philosopher Maurice Friedman recently wrote: "Now Martin Buber
and Carl Rogers are dead, but even after 30 years, the issues raised in
their dialogue still seem to me momentous" (1994, p. 47). If the ideas
expressed in the dialogue approach this level of importance, and we
think they do, then students of dialogue should be confident that the
historical record is accurate, and must be assured that commentaries—
previous and subsequent—invoke as much relevant context as possible
for Buber's and Rogers's remarks. This new annotated transcript corrects
many major and minor errors that mar extant transcripts, and elaborates

1

essential context for understanding this vital conversation in the history of ideas. Previous interpretations and nearly four decades of scholarly quotation have placed virtually complete trust on a transcript of somewhat uncertain origin, which was—to be generous—inexact. In subsequent reprints, many changes to the transcript were justified on criteria of readability; but these, too, take a reader even further from the actual conversation and often alter connotations significantly.

Martin Buber and Carl Rogers met for over an hour of public dialogue on April 18, 1957. Buber, the renowned Jewish philosopher of dialogue, was 79 and on his second trip to the United States. He was invited by Leslie Farber to deliver a series of lectures at the Washington School of Psychiatry, and Rev. DeWitt C. Baldwin, Coordinator of Religious Affairs at the University of Michigan, took the opportunity to invite Buber to his campus for a three-day conference in Buber's honor, the "Mid-West Conference with Dr. Martin Buber" (see "Program," 1957). For Thursday evening, the second day of the conference, Baldwin planned a dialogue between Buber and the American humanistic psychologist and psychotherapist Carl Rogers. Rogers, at 55, was well known among psychologists for his development of a "client-centered" theory of psychotherapy and for his skill as an interviewer and facilitator. They were joined on the stage by Maurice Friedman, then a young professor of philosophy at Sarah Lawrence College, an acknowledged authority on Buber's thought who had devoted several pages of his *Martin Buber: The Life of Dialogue* (1955b) to exploring similarities between Buber's philosophy and Rogers's approach to psychotherapy. This evening would be the only meeting between these two seminal thinkers, whose ideas on "the nature of man as revealed in inter-personal relationship"[1] have been compared so often. Surely no one could have predicted the long-term significance of the Buber-Rogers conversation that evening.[2]

---

1. "The nature of man as revealed in inter-personal relationship" was the general topic of the dialogue suggested by Rogers and conveyed to Buber by Baldwin (Baldwin, 1957c, 1957d).

2. Surely Buber did not. He declined to allow his lectures and seminars at the Washington School of Psychiatry, which he gave at the outset of this trip, to be filmed, despite his host having arranged a large grant and secured the services of a well known documentary film-maker, because to do so "slackens the spontaneity" (Buber, 1957a, 1991, p. 605) that he regarded as essential for dialogue, and on arrival in the United States even refused to have these sessions audio-recorded (Friedman, 1983, pp. 210–211; 1991, pp. 361–362).

Interpreters of Buber and Rogers refer often to the dialogue to discuss the thought of one or the other or to distinguish between them (Anderson, 1982; Arnett, 1981, 1982, 1986, 1989; Brace, 1992; Brink, 1987; Burstow, 1987; Friedman, 1983, 1985, 1986, 1992; Kelb, 1991; Peterson, 1976; Rasmussen, 1991; Rendahl, 1975; Roffey, 1980; Schaeder, 1973; Thorne, 1992; Upshaw, 1970; Van Balen, 1990; Van Belle, 1980; Yocum, 1980). In addition, Friedman (1994), Seckinger (1976), Thorne (1992), and Yoshida (1994) have directly analyzed the dialogue itself. All of these discussions appear to presume that Buber and Rogers engaged in a spontaneous and unrehearsed dialogue in which both partners were equally able to articulate their ideas. Returning to the taped dialogue itself, and reconsidering what Buber and Rogers actually said, casts doubt on this presumption in a variety of ways we will explore in our commentary.

Another reflection of the significance of the dialogue is that four somewhat variant transcripts of it have been published in English.[3] Very seldom are intellectual dialogues even transcribed, much less repeatedly reprinted and analyzed in the scholarly literature. Unfortunately, all published transcripts of this event (Buber, 1965b, pp. 166–184; "Dialogue Between," 1960; Friedman, 1964; Kirschenbaum & Henderson, 1989,

---

The organizers of the Buber conference in Michigan, of which the dialogue with Rogers was a part, hoped that they could record the dialogue and had made arrangements with audio-visual services at the university to do so. Although the equipment was in place in advance, they did not know until a few minutes before the dialogue that Buber had agreed to have a recording made.

Grey Austin, then Assistant Coordinator of Religious Affairs at the University of Michigan and the person responsible for arranging many of the details of the conference, reported to us that, during the hour or so when Buber and Rogers met immediately prior to the dialogue, Rogers convinced Buber to allow the taping (Austin, personal communication, January 1, 1996, February 12, 1996). Rogers, he believes, assured Buber that he regularly recorded therapy sessions without any interruption to that sensitive process and that his office had the expertise to transcribe a recording faithfully. Maurice Friedman, who moderated the dialogue, told us that he thought Buber agreed to this taping although refusing at the Washington School of Psychiatry because he had such low expectations for his dialogue with Rogers (Friedman, personal communication, October 22, 1991). This also seems reasonable because Buber believed public dialogue, such as the one with Rogers that involved a large audience, to be impossible, almost a contradiction in terms.

3. In addition, a translation of the transcript from Buber (1965b) has been published in German ("Dialogue zwischen," 1992).

pp. 42–63) have significant and serious errors because all were based on the same typescript made shortly after the dialogue ("Dialogue Between," nd; "Dialogue Between," 1957–60). That typescript, originally circulated by Rogers, was flawed, and none of the subsequent published transcripts (nor any of the discussions of the dialogue mentioned above) seem to have relied on a fresh listening to the audiotape itself. This is an issue we consider in more detail later.

This dialogue is also mentioned significantly in biographies of Buber and of Rogers. Maurice Friedman's definitive three-volume and single-volume biographies of Buber analyze the dialogue at some length (1983, pp. 208, 225–227, 254, 257–258; 1991, pp. 368–370) as do his commentaries on Buber's thought cited above. Kirschenbaum's (1979) biography of Rogers, oddly enough, mentions the dialogue only very briefly (p. 393), although in Russell's oral history interviews with Rogers and in Thorne's recent book the dialogue is discussed much more prominently (Rogers & Russell, 1991, pp. 201–202; Thorne, 1992, esp. pp. 69–89). Rogers also referred to the dialogue occasionally (1960, p. 96; 1969, p. 349; 1980, p. 9), and even quoted from it in one of his most famous essays (1961, pp. 55, 57). In his interview with Richard Evans (Evans, 1975), Rogers described the dialogue with Buber as "very meaningful to both of us" (p. 111). Although Buber never explicitly wrote about the dialogue, he described it as a "memorable occasion" (Friedman, 1957); and Friedman implies that a section of Buber's famous "Postscript" to the 1958 edition of *I and Thou* (see pp. 177–179) was at least in part a response to the dialogue with Rogers (Friedman, 1983, pp. 254–255).

The general public was invited to the dialogue, which was held in the most beautiful and prestigious auditorium on the University of Michigan campus, Rackham Auditorium. Although scheduled to last only one hour, it continued for over an hour and a half. Other notables participating in the conference included the economist Kenneth Boulding; Perry LeFevre and Ross Snyder of the Divinity School at the University of Chicago; Bill McKeachie of the Center for Teaching and Learning at the University of Michigan; the anthropologist Dorothy Lee; and literary critic R. W. B. Lewis, then of Rutgers ("Attendence" [*sic*], nd; Friedman, 1983, p. 225; 1991, p. 368; "Program," 1957). The audience for the dialogue also included Judith Buber Agassi, Buber's grand-daughter, herself now a noted sociologist, and Buber's wife, Paula.

DeWitt Baldwin had corresponded with Buber and Rogers about arrangements and the topic the men would discuss (Baldwin, 1957a, 1957b, 1957c, 1957d). One of Rogers's suggestions, "the nature of man as revealed in inter-personal relationship" (Baldwin, 1957c, 1957d), was adopted as the general topic for the dialogue. Baldwin also determined the participants' roles (Friedman, personal communication, December 14, 1991) as described by Friedman in his preliminary remarks that evening—"And the form of this dialogue will be that Dr. Rogers will himself raise questions with Dr. Buber and Dr. Buber will respond, and perhaps with a question, perhaps with a statement" (from our transcript of the dialogue, Turn 2). We have argued elsewhere (Anderson & Cissna, 1991, 1996b; Cissna & Anderson, 1994, 1996) that recognizing the roles assigned to the participants and the presence of two nonparticipating audiences[4] are essential to understanding this encounter.

Eventually, the tape recorder did bring a larger audience to their dialogue. Having facilities for transcribing therapeutic interviews, we suspect that Rogers volunteered to produce a transcript of the dialogue.[5] We do not know who actually did the work or what Rogers's personal role in producing the transcript might have been. He first circulated the transcript, and sent a copy to Buber in January, 1958, as a "token by which to recall our few moments of dialogue" (Rogers, 1958a).[6]

A transcript of the interchange was first published in 1960 in a Japanese psychology journal, *Psychologia* ("Dialogue Between," 1960), and was introduced only by the four sentences that headed the original typescript.[7] While providing no clues to how the manuscript came to be submitted or invited, the editor's note at the beginning of that issue of

---

4. The 400 people present that evening were the immediate audience, while the more distant and far larger potential audience was represented by the tape recorder.

5. Rogers's brief notes on the back of his conference program include "Ask Baldwin re. tape" as well as Buber's address—written in Buber's handwriting ("Tentative Program," 1957). Rogers pioneered recording and transcribing psychotherapy interviews (see 1942b) and published the first complete transcript of a psychotherapy case (see Rogers, 1942a). We should not be surprised, therefore, that Rogers would volunteer in 1957 to produce a transcript of this dialogue.

6. The original typescript as well as a single mimeographed copy are preserved in the Carl R. Rogers Collection at the Library of Congress. Rogers's use of the word "moments" here, while probably innocent, may have been a pointed reference echoing the interchange within the dialogue about whether therapeutic mutuality is ongoing or a matter of intense moments. We know that Buber received the typescript because Grete Schaeder later indicated that Buber loaned it to her (Schaeder, 1973, p. 480).

7. "A Mid-West Conference on Martin Buber was organized by the University of Michigan in April, 1957, during Dr. Buber's visit to this country, arranged by the William Alanson White Foundation. The famous philosopher from the University of Jerusalem gave several lectures during the three-day

the journal implied that both Rogers and Buber agreed to its publication.[8] An abbreviated version of the transcript next appeared in Friedman's critical reader, *The Worlds of Existentialism* (1964, pp. 485–497). The most accessible and commonly cited transcript was published the next year as an appendix to Buber's *The Knowledge of Man* (1965b), edited by Friedman. The most recent transcript in English was printed in Kirschenbaum and Henderson's (1989, pp. 41–63) collection of dialogues Rogers held with noted intellectuals.[9] This transcript was reprinted from the *Psychologia* transcript, with minor changes in punctuation and spelling, corrections of a few printing errors, and the omission of one word. Recently, a translation of the transcript from *The Knowledge of Man* appeared in German ("Dialog zwischen," 1992). All of these transcripts are based on the original typescript circulated by Rogers, and none show evidence that those reprinting the transcripts systematically listened to the audiotape to compare it with what they printed.

In all likelihood, the initial transcribing was done by a secretary working for Rogers.[10] We know that Rogers listened carefully to the tape and made six pages of extensive notes (Rogers, nd-b). We do not know whether he personally compared the completed transcript with the tape. Only Friedman (see Buber, 1965b, p. 166) acknowledged editing the transcript, although he later referred to what he produced as a "verbatim"

---

conference, using papers he had delivered in Washington as the William Alanson White Memorial lectures.

"Another feature of the program at Ann Arbor was a dialogue on April 18, between Dr. Buber and Dr. Carl Rogers, Professor of Psychology and Executive Secretary of the Counseling Center, University of Chicago. This dialogue was recorded, and because of numerous requests, a transcription of it is presented here" ("Dialogue Between," nd, p. 1; "Dialogue Between," 1957–60, p. 1; "Dialogue Between," 1960, p. 208).

8. "It is a great pleasure for us and would be so for our readers as well that we can publish a dialogue between Prof. Martin Buber and Prof. Carl Rogers in this issue *by their favor*" (Sato, 1960; emphasis added).

9. Following Buber (in 1957), Rogers later held public dialogues with B. F. Skinner (in 1962), Paul Tillich (in 1965), Michael Polanyi (in 1966), and Gregory Bateson (in 1975).

10. Several sources, including a long-time secretary of Rogers from the early 1950s (personal communication, Mrs. Dorothy Becker, October 18, 1995), affirm that it was Rogers's practice to employ secretaries to transcribe tapes of therapy sessions. As secretaries were experienced at the task of transcribing, it is very likely that one or more secretarial employees transcribed the tape of the dialogue.

record (Friedman, 1983, p. 225). Although he claimed to have made only "very minor editorial changes and deletions" intended to "facilitate readability" while changing "nothing of substance," whether he fulfilled that promise depends on what is defined as substantial. We believe some relatively significant changes were made. Friedman has used the dialogue to clarify aspects of Buber's thought. Our interest is different: We see the dialogue as instrumental in *influencing* the thought of the two men and as instrumental in illustrating if not redirecting some basic assumptions of the human sciences. We are interested, therefore, in studying the *process* of the dialogue through which and from which such changes developed. For Friedman, any editing that clarifies or sharpens Buber's ideas is useful; for us, that same editing may obscure important aspects of the interactional process.

We have not been able to learn much about the audiotape itself. We do not know the kind of machine on which it was originally recorded, although the work was done with portable equipment by the audio-visual department at the University.[11] We do not know exactly when the machine was turned on (our most complete copy begins after Baldwin started his introduction, and apparently no recording was made while the tape was being changed in the middle of the dialogue). We do not know for certain what generation our tapes are, although we believe the best one is a first-generation copy of the original, which is what DeWitt C. Baldwin, Jr., believes he donated to the Humanistic Psychology Archive at the University of California at Santa Barbara. We do not know for certain the quality of the original recording, nor do we know the kind of the equipment used to make the original transcript. Nevertheless, despite the inevitable degradation of fidelity associated with tape transfers, we found both of our better recordings to be quite clear and (usually) distinct.[12]

Our transcript was produced with a Lanier VoiceWriter 105 (Model P-148) audiocassette transcribing machine and Maxell UR90 (IEC Type I)

---

11. In response to requests over the years, Rogers occasionally sent people the tape recording along with the transcript, but he recommended the transcript because the tape, he said, is "quite hard to understand" (Rogers, 1977). In one letter, he noted that although the recording was done by the Michigan Audio-Visual Bureau (presumably a department of the University of Michigan), he thought that "they didn't do a very good job of it" (Rogers, 1959b).

12. Contemporary audio equipment may be enough better that we are able to decipher utterances that could not be understood on playback machines from nearly forty years ago.

audiotape. The recorder gave us extensive control over tape speed, tone, and volume, and allowed adjustable recall for listening to a single word, phrase, or sentence many times. In addition, some portions of the transcript were verified using a high-quality Yamaha KX 1200 cassette deck and Sennheiser HD 540 Reference headphones.

We attempted to produce an accurate *reader's* transcript, not one that would satisfy the stricter criteria of conversation analysis. We listened to the tape many times, gradually improving and correcting the transcript. Using the recall feature, we were able to listen to some particularly difficult words and phrases literally scores of times. We asked others to listen to the tape or different sections of it with us—a research assistant, departmental colloquium audiences, graduate and undergraduate seminars, and an audience member from the original dialogue who was familiar with the thought of both Buber and Rogers (Dr. Seymour Cain).

During the past several years, while refining the transcript, we pursued several allied projects: studying how the interpersonal issues of role, audience, and interpersonal style contributed to the conversation; investigating necessary and appropriate dimensions of a rhetorical approach to conversation; considering the implications of this historical event for contemporary issues in public dialogue; and fleshing out historical details of the dialogue. As our interests evolved, we continued to consider how to present the transcript, and have come to believe that the differences between the previously published transcripts and what we heard on the audiotape justify publication of a new and more accurate transcript. At the same time, many readers will be interested in the intellectual context for this conversation. We have added, therefore, the kind of limited commentary that could point readers to key issues and sources without, we hope, overwhelming the ideas themselves.

All of the transcripts, including the original typescript circulated by Rogers, contain a myriad of inaccuracies. They omit many, but not all, contextual references to the audience, circumstances, and event; omit participation by the audience (in the form of laughter, applause, and offering suggestions for a word); and ignore the principals' own laughter as well. The transcripts eliminate most interruptions and virtually all vocal encouragers and interjected comments. The transcripts include very few of the many lengthy pauses, and often pauses that are noted are placed incorrectly. The transcripts reflect changes—small and large—in what Buber and Rogers said (additions, deletions, and substitutions)— often in an apparent attempt to aid readability, reduce ambiguity, or increase sense. These attempts were frequently unsuccessful and were sometimes inappropriate. We found several occasions in which the changes altered Buber's and Rogers's comments from clarity to confusion and resolved ambiguities inappropriately or erroneously. Frequently, vocal emphasis was not noted or was placed incorrectly. Perhaps most disturbing, we also found a significant number of cases in which the transcriber simply misheard what was said.

Several points about our transcript and commentary are worth noting in advance:

1. The speaking turns are numbered in order (from 1 to 128) and the commentary paragraphs numbered to correspond with the speaking turns.

2. Hundreds of small changes (such as hesitations, repetitions, minor word adjustments, and vocal inflection) are, of course, reflected in the transcript, but not discussed in the commentary for reasons of space.

3. We have organized the dialogue into eight parts, corresponding to the opening and closing remarks and six numbered questions—the first four questions Rogers asked of Buber and the final two questions asked by Friedman. Interestingly, Rogers's notes from the dialogue, presumably made shortly afterwards, are also organized by the six major questions.

4. The extant transcripts are designated in our discussion as CR (the original typescript circulated by Rogers, an original of which is found in the Library of Congress), P (the *Psychologia* version based on the CR typescript), MF (a partial transcript published in Friedman's *The Worlds of Existentialism*), B-F (the transcript published in Buber's *The Knowledge of Man*, based on P and to which Friedman made "very minor editorial changes and deletions to facilitate the readability of the dialogue, but . . . changed nothing of substance"), and K-H (the transcript published in Kirschenbaum and Henderson's *Carl Rogers: Dialogues*, essentially reprinted from P.

5. With few exceptions, there are only two basic previous transcripts: (a) the original typescript, published in *Psychologia* and reprinted in Kirschenbaum and Henderson, and (b) the transcript edited by Friedman for *The Knowledge of Man*. When we mention "previous" or "existing" transcripts generically in our analysis, it is to these two basic versions that we refer.

Transcript of the Dialogue,
with Commentary

Opening

1. REV. DEWITT BALDWIN: [most of the first 11 seconds on the tape are unintelligible] . . . Dr. Maurice Friedman as a, well, interpreter or moderator . . . and I'm sure that many of you have been looking forward to this opportunity of um seeing the exchange and feeling the [unintelligible] that the two men like Dr. Carl Rogers and Dr. Buber. And uh uh so my uh job tonight is a very pleasant one in [quality of recording improves] bidding you welcome and saying sit back and enjoy uh at least an hour of time when you can think with two men who uh want to come to little closer grips with with their own ideas. Uh, I I just want to introduce one person and let then let him uh speak of the others. Uh, the moderator is Professor Maurice S. Friedman, professor of uh philosophy at Sarah Lawrence College, Bronxville, New York. Professor Friedman uh, as those who have been in the conference well realize, is one of the best American inter-

1. Transcription: This version of Baldwin's introduction is longer and more detailed than the one in the original typescript (located in the Carl R. Rogers Collection at the Library of Congress, Washington, D.C.), which was reprinted in the P and K-H transcripts but omitted in the most frequently cited transcript (B-F).

13

preters of Martin Buber. He had his undergraduate work at Harvard, graduate work at Ohio State and the University of Chicago, where he took his doctor's degree, and perhaps is best known in relation to Martin Buber for his book, *Martin Buber: The Life of Dialogue*. And uh so, uh, Maurice, I'll turn over to you and uh know you'll have a good time.

2. MAURICE FRIEDMAN: Thank you, DeWitt Baldwin. Gives me a great deal of pleasure to moderate this because I could say I perhaps initiated the the dialogue between Professor Buber and and Professor Rogers some years ago when someone pointed out to me some resemblances in, in their thought, and I wrote to Dr. Rogers and he kindly supplied me with some papers and then we corresponded a while, and then I sent this material to to Buber, including some of uh Professor Rogers's articles, and so I was very happy indeed when uh the idea of the two of them speaking here in dialogue came up. I think it is a a *most* significant meeting, not just in terms of uh—[brief largely unintelligible interruption apparently having to do with the position of the microphone] not just in terms of psychotherapy, but of the fact that both these men have [unintel-

2. Transcription: The B-F transcript shortens the last part of Friedman's description of roles by omitting how Buber would respond to Rogers's questions.
Content/Process: (a) Friedman clearly delineates the significance of the meeting of these two seminal thinkers, but emphasizes the central role of Buber, as the conference has been organized around him. (b) "The form of this dialogue" stipulation is a crucial feature of the meeting that has been neglected by other studies. It creates both ground rules to guide the talk and roles to guide the participants and audience—making the dialogue more of an "interview" on stage (Anderson & Cissna, 1996b; Cissna & Anderson, 1994). (c) Although not mentioned in the introduction, apparently the principals had also agreed not to allow questions from the audience (Friedman, 1983, p. 225; 1991, p. 368).[13]

---

13. According to Maurice Friedman, the principals agreed in advance that there would be no questions from the audience, and we note that neither

ligible] our admiration as persons
with an approach to uh personal
relations and personal becoming.
There are so many remarkable
similarities between their thought
that it's also intriguing to to have
the privilege of seeing them talk
with one another and seeing what
issues may also come out. And my
role as moderator is only, uh, if
occasion should arise, to sharpen
these issues or interpret one way
or another. Um, you don't, I think,
need introduction to Professor
Buber since the conference is centered around him, and I'm sure
you don't need introduction to Dr.
Rogers either. He is the, of course,
has been famous for a great many
years as the founder of the once
so- so-called nondirective therapy,
now, I believe, rechristened client-
centered therapy, and is the
Director of the University of
Chicago Counseling Center, where
he has had very fruitful relations
with the uh theological group and
the uh personality and religion uh
courses there. And the form of this
dialogue will be that Dr. Rogers
will himself raise questions with
Dr. Buber and Dr. Buber will
respond, and perhaps with a question, perhaps with a statement.
We'll let them carry it from there.
Dr. Rogers.

Friedman nor Baldwin, in their introductions, mentioned any opportunity
for questions. However, one member of the audience with whom we spoke
(Rev. Russell J. Becker, November 29, 1995) had a vivid recall of a brief
question-and-answer period. No other audience members we talked with
had any recollection about this one way or the other.

I

Invitation and Stories

3. CARL R. ROGERS: One thing I think I would say to the audience before starting to talk with Dr. Buber is that this is most certainly an unrehearsed dialogue. Uh, the weather made it necessary for me to spend all day arriving here, uh, and so it was only an hour or two ago that I met Dr. Buber, even though I have met him a long time ago in his writings.

I think that the, uh, first question I would like to ask you, Dr. Buber, um, may sound a trifle impertinent, but I would like to explain it and then perhaps it won't seem impertinent. I have wondered: How have you lived so deeply in interpersonal relationships and gained such an understanding of the human individual, without being a psychotherapist? Um. [Buber laughs; audience laughs] The uh, now the the reason I ask that is that it seems to me that a number of us have come to sense and experience some of the same kinds of learnings that

3. Transcription: (a) The B-F transcript deletes Rogers's reference to the audience and to the bad weather that forced him to arrive just shortly before the dialogue. These comments, while less relevant to the intellectual substance of the dialogue, established an interpersonal immediacy that is quite relevant for understanding the interaction process. (b) Somewhat arbitrarily, we have chosen to note pauses of 2.5 seconds or more.

Content/Process: (a) Rogers from the beginning establishes the presence and importance of an audience, as well as the unrehearsed nature of the interaction. Perhaps in part responding to Friedman's comments about participants' roles, Rogers appeared to be reassuring the audience that they would not be observing a rehearsed or staged event, but a free-flowing conversation. Rogers had in fact prepared nine possible questions for Buber, four of

you have expressed in your writings, but very frequently we have come to those learnings through our experience in psychotherapy. I think that there is something about um the therapeutic relationship that gives us permission, almost *formal* permission, to enter into a deep and close relationship with a person, and so we tend to learn very deeply in that way. I think of one uh psychiatrist friend of mine who says that [2.5 second pause—hereafter noted only by the length of time in seconds indicated in brackets] he never feels as whole, or as much of a person, as he does in his therapeutic interviews; and I, I share that feeling. And so, um, if it is not too personal, I, I would be interested in knowing what were the the channels of knowing that enabled you to, to really learn so deeply of of people and of relationships?

which he actually used,[14] a fact that no previous commentary has acknowledged. Rogers's own notes confirm that in his opening question, the phrase, "trifle impertinent" was planned, not an ad lib. To have prepared questions, which functioned as "openers" to his conversation with Buber, is entirely consistent with Rogers's assurance to the audience that the conversation was not rehearsed. This was advertised as a "dialogue," and Rogers is cuing the audience—and Buber—that he takes that charge seriously and that whatever ensued, successful or not, the possibility of genuine dialogue was present. (b) Rogers's initial phrasing of his question might "sound a trifle impertinent" because it presumes through friendly irony that his own profession is a primary avenue of knowing and understanding human behavior, and that

---

14. Rogers's notes for all the questions were extensive, and frequently included quoted passages either from his own writing or Buber's. The questions not asked were initially numbered four, six, seven, eight, and nine, and concerned: (4) whether Buber's concept of inclusion (Rogers noted a passage from "Education" in *Between Man and Man*) implies that the "basic nature [of human beings] is positive"; (6) how Buber conceives "of the way in which human beings change in a therapeutic or I-Thou relationship" and how this compares to the "elements of the process of change as I see them and have tried to describe them in a recent paper" (which seemed to be what became chapter 8 of *On Becoming a Person*); (7) whether Buber agrees that a person, relationship, nation, or scientific field is "best or soundest or most effective, when it is in the process of becoming"; (8) how Buber conceives of teaching and learning and whether he agrees that all "significant learning" is "self-appropriated" and "cannot be taught"; and (9) whether Buber feels "there is danger in the world of I-It, in the form of the behavioral sciences, encroaching on the world of I-Thou" (Rogers, 1957a).

Buber came to similar knowing—as Friedman noted in his introduction—through other routes. In asking his question in this way, Rogers establishes his own experiential base, implicates other psychotherapists and a psychiatrist in support of his "learnings," and (relevant to a later exchange) suggests that the therapist—in addition to the client—is helped by the therapeutic relationship. This facet of the question also reminded us of Jacob Bronowski's remark to the effect that an impertinent question will often open the doors to a pertinent answer (from Rieber, 1989, p. 1); and if Rogers's question might be termed impertinent, as we will see, it certainly brought forth a highly pertinent answer from Buber. (c) Although Rogers labels his question as impertinent, by offering that label and by the way he asks the question, he deflects the possibility that it would be understood as truly impertinent. Rogers is genuinely interested—and no doubt thinks the audience will be too—in how Buber's philosophy of dialogue developed. The numerous pauses—both the longer ones we have noted and the many shorter ones we haven't—indicate something of Rogers's thoughtfulness and his interest in having Buber appreciate the ground of the question. (d) In concluding his question, Rogers invites a personal answer from Buber, while also inviting Buber to set his own limits for the dialogue's personal tone.

4. MARTIN BUBER: Hmmm. Er, It's rather a biographical question. Eh, eh, I think I must give instead of one answer, two. [Rogers: Uhm huh] One, eh, eh, [unclear: "aber" (German for "but") or perhaps "rather"]—this is only just a particular—is that I'm not eh entirely a stranger in, eh, let me say, psychiatry [Rogers: Uhm huh], because when I was a student—it's long ago—I hmm studied three terms uh psychiatry, and uh what eh they call in Germany "Psychiatrische-Klinique." [Rogers: Uh huh] Uh. I was just, eh I was most interested in the latter. You see, I have not studied psychiatry in order to become [Rogers: Hm hmm] a psychotherapist. I studied it, eh, three terms. First uh with eh Flechsig in Leipzig, uh, where I was eh, eh student of Wundt's, Wundt. [Rogers: Uh huh] Eh, afterwards in Berlin eh with Mendel, and third term with eh Bleuler in Zurich [Rogers: Uh huh], which was the most interesting of the three. Eh, and, eh, I wanted just uh then, [unintelligible—German phrase?] I also was a very young, inexperienced, and not eh very, not very understanding young man. But I had the, had the feeling that I wanted to know about eh man, eh and eh man in the *so-called* pathological state. I doubted even then if it is the right term. [Rogers: Oh, I see] Eh, I wanted to eh to see, if possible to meet, such people, and to establish—as far as I can remember—to establish the

4.   Transcription: Numerous details in this statement have been misheard, misnoted, or curiously edited. (a) The CR and P transcripts have only a blank line for "Flechsig," indicating that the word was unintelligible; Friedman inserted "Flechsig" in his B-F transcript, and corrected the spelling of "Mendel." Interestingly, existing transcripts have Buber saying only that there were students of Wundt in Leipzig while Buber was there—although Buber states that he himself was a student of Wundt (see Friedman, 1981, pp. 22, 24; 1991, pp. 14–15). Schaeder (1973, p. 203) describes Buber as telling Rogers that he took part in "some psychological laboratory experiments" under Wundt, which he may have, but it wasn't part of what he said to Rogers. This is especially intriguing because the transcripts to which Schaeder had access— Buber had loaned her the typescript that Rogers had sent him (p. 480) and she also had the B-F transcript in *The Knowledge of Man*— had Buber saying only that there were students of Wundt in Leipzig while he was there. (b) A long pause by Buber (almost six seconds) was, significantly, respected by Rogers without interruption, but is not noted at all in previous transcripts—although an ellipsis was inappropriately inserted at a later point where there was virtually no pause. (c) Existing transcripts have Buber saying that he "began as a young man," which

relation, the real relation between what we call a sane man and what we call a pathological man. [Rogers: Uh huh] And this I have learned in some uh measure—as far as eh a boy of uh twenty or so can [Buber chuckles] can learn such things.

Eh, but what *mainly* uh constituted what you ask, is—it was something other. It was just hmm a certain eh inclination to eh meet people, and as far as possible to, just to [5.7] change if possible something in the other, *but also* to let me be changed by him. Eh, at any event, I had no resistance—I put no resistance [Rogers: Uh huh] to it. [Rogers: Uh huh] I eh—already then as a young man—I felt I have not the right to want to change another if I am not open to be changed by him as far as it is legitimate. Something is to be changed and his touch, his contact, is able to change it more or less. I cannot eh be, so to say, above him, and say, "No! I'm out of the play. [Rogers: Uh huh] Uh, you are mad." [Rogers: Uh huh] And so eh from my—let me see—there were, there are two phases of it. The first phase went til the year eighteen, eighteen nineteen, uh meaning til my, til I was eh about forty.

makes no sense in this context, instead of what he actually said, which was that "already then as a young man" he felt he hadn't the right to change another unilaterally. (d) Previous transcripts refer to the "concept" of the other when Buber said "contact," extending his "touch" metaphor. (e) Here and in turn 6, the B-F transcript corrects Buber's mistakes identifying dates. (f) Within this turn we hear the first instance of an interjected comment from the other, in this case from Rogers. While these are, obviously, not substantively meaningful turns, and were omitted in other transcripts, we note them to indicate the extent to which the speakers reinforced and were attentive to each other. (g) Seymour Cain, who was at the dialogue, listened to some of the tape with us and was the first to suggest that Buber may have used a German word in this response (personal communication, August 10, 1993).
Content/Process: (a) In labeling this a "biographical question," Buber may have been considering how to respond to this query. He did not like biographical questions that were intended to reduce philosophy to biography or to interpret ideas in light of the life experiences of a thinker. As it turned out, Buber was quite willing to discuss with Rogers, and occasionally to write about (see Buber, 1973), the experiences from which his philosophy emerged; but only a few years earlier he had declined to respond

at all to questions from a young doctoral student about his early family life (Buber, 1952a; Friedman, 1983, pp. 186–187). (b) By not interrupting a quite lengthy pause, by respectfully maintaining Buber's "floor," Rogers in effect verified for Buber and the audience that the evening's focus was to remain on Buber. (c) Buber's statement that he felt he didn't have "the right to want to change another if I am not open to be changed by him as far as it is legitimate" seems very close to the kind of mutuality or equality that Rogers later in this conversation suggested were characteristic of his experience in therapeutic relations. In response to that, however, Buber asserted that the limits placed on such a relationship precluded mutuality. We note that although this dialogue has been quoted to illustrate Buber's thought on mutuality, his statements on this topic from later in the dialogue have usually been removed from the context of these earlier comments.

5.   ROGERS: Hm-hmm. Till you're about forty? Uh hum.

6.   BUBER: Just so. [Rogers: Hmm] And eh [3.0] then I, in eighteen nineteen, I felt something rather strange. I felt that I had been, been eh strongly influenced by something that came to an end just then, meaning eh the Second, the First World War.

5, 7.   Transcription: These turns are deleted in previous transcripts.
Content/Process: By clarifying Buber's inconsistent dates for himself and the audience without correcting or even directly questioning Buber about them, Rogers contributed to establishing a respectful and nonjudgmental tone to the evening.

7. ROGERS: In in nineteen eighteen.

8. BUBER: M-hmmm. [Rogers: M-hmmm] It ended then, and in the course of the war, I did not feel very much about this influence. But at the end I felt, "Oh, I have been terribly influenced," because I eh [3.1] could not resist to what went on, and I was just compelled to, may I say so, to live it. You see? Uh, things that went on uh just in this moment. [Rogers: Uh huh] Eh, you uh you may call it "imagining the real." [Rogers: Uh huh] Imagining what was going on. This is—this imagining, eh, for four years [Rogers: Hmmm], eh, influenced me terribly. Just when it was finished [Rogers: Uh hmm], eh it finished by a certain episode uh in uh May nineteen when a friend of mine, a great friend, a great man, was killed by, by uh, antirevolutionary soldiers [Rogers: Uh huh] in a very barbaric way, and I, now again once more—and this was the last time—I was eh compelled to imagine eh just this eh killing, but not in an optical way alone, but may I say so, just with my body.

8. Transcription: The CR and P transcripts have "*imagining the real*," as though two words were emphasized. Friedman (B-F), however, realizing that this is a significant concept of Buber's (e.g., see 1965a, pp. 96–101), italicized the entire phrase. Because there was little vocal emphasis, however, we have employed quotation marks to suggest its conceptual meaning to Buber.

Content/Process: This incident concerning the "great friend," Gustav Landauer, is an autobiographical event that preoccupied Buber and about which he felt "too close" ever to be able to write (in Buber, 1973, p. 8). Friedman describes it as one of the three most important events in Buber's life (see Friedman, 1981, 257–258; 1991, pp. 114–115). Apparently this was the only occasion in which Buber spoke or wrote publicly about the impact of this episode on him. This kind of emotional revelation is naturally one of the goals of an effective interviewer; Rogers's (impertinent) question and curiosity has stimulated Buber to voice a real but dormant experience.

9. ROGERS: With your feelings.

9. Transcription: This turn is deleted in previous transcripts.

10. BUBER: And this was the decisive [unintelligible] or rather

10. Transcription: Where previous transcripts have "many con-

eh the decisive moment, after which, after some days and nights eh in this eh state, I eh felt, "Oh, something has been done to me." [Rogers: Uh huh] And from then on, eh, eh, these meetings with people, particularly with young, young people um were the eh— became—in a somewhat different form. I had a decisive experience, experience of four years, very concrete experience, and eh from now on, I had to give something eh more than just eh eh my inclination to eh exchange eh-eh thoughts and feelings, and so on. Eh, I had to give the fruit of an experience.

crete experiences," we heard "very concrete experience."

Content/Process: Buber here provides personal historical context for the difference between mere exchange and offering the dialogic "fruit of an experience," a distinction he developed in depth in his writing.

11.   ROGERS: M-hmmm, m-hmmm. Sounds as though you're saying the the knowledge, perhaps, or some of it, came in the twenties, but then some of the wisdom you have about uh interpersonal relationships came from wanting to meet people openly without wanting to dominate. And then—I see this as kind of a threefold answer—and then third, from really living the World War, but living it in your own feelings and [Buber: Uh huh] imagination.

11.   Transcription: In this summary, Rogers notes that Buber's knowledge came in "the twenties" rather than in "your twenties," as previous transcripts have it. However, obviously, he is referring to Buber's age, rather than to the 1920s.

Content/Process: This is a prototypical Rogers "perception check" or "reflection," an example of what he calls "active listening." Rogers (Rogers & Farson, 1957) had just recently coauthored his famous exposition on this listening style, and its emphasis on the meaning of the other was probably in the forefront of his mind. Rogers here organizes and clarifies Buber's answer effectively—perhaps as much for the audience as for himself—without trying to reply to it.

12. BUBER: Hmm. Just so. [Rogers: Huh hm] Because this eh latter was really, I cannot eh-eh say it in another language, it was really a living *with* those people. People wounded, killed [Rogers: Uhm huh] in the war.

13. ROGERS: You you felt their wounds.

14. BUBER: Yes. But feeling is not sufficiently strong—[Rogers: Ah, uh huh]—the word "feeling."

15. ROGERS: Uh huh, you'd like something stronger.

I'm going to make one suggestion, even though it interrupts us a little. I can't face the mike and face you at the same time. [Buber: Oh] Would you mind if I turned the table just a little?

16. BUBER: Yes, please, please do.

17. ROGERS: Then I—

18. BUBER: Shall I sit here?

19. ROGERS: Yes. It—move it forward just a little then I think it uh—

20. BUBER: Is this right?

21. ROGERS: That seems better to me. Hope it does to the audience.

12. Transcription: Although previous transcripts have Buber emphasizing "living," instead he clearly emphasizes "with." This emphasis, of course, is consistent with his own philosophy of "the between."

Content/Process: Buber, by emphasizing "with" in this statement, previews his later points about inclusion and "imagining the real."

15. Transcription: (a) The CR and P transcripts delete Rogers's "Uh huh, you'd like something stronger," a perception check similar in function to his earlier comment in turn 13, "You you felt their wounds." (b) The B-F transcript deletes the entire episode of Rogers's attempt to move the table to facilitate interaction (turns 15–21).

Content/Process: Rogers takes primary responsibility for the communicative process by adjusting their physical environment to allow better interaction. In doing so, he indicates not only his role as questioner-respondent but his concern for the audience ("That seems better to me. Hope it does to the audience" [Turn 21]). The P transcript, which reports these turns, deletes this reference to the audience. Although such deletions are trivial in the sense that they don't directly affect the flow of ideas, they are revealing for students of communication process who are interested in the impact of roles and the negotiation of relationships.

22. FRIEDMAN: While he is uh changing, I'll interject this, that Professor Rogers's question reminded me of uh a a theological student from a Baptist seminary who talked to me about Professor Buber's thought for an hour, and when he left he said, "I must ask you this question. Professor Buber is so good. How is it he's not a Christian?" [Laughter]

22. Transcription: (a) Friedman "interjects" his story, rather than "admitting" it, as other transcripts have it. (b) We have used the standard convention in scholarly writing of creating a possessive from a name ending with "s"; the CR and P transcripts use "Rogers'," while the B-F text contains the typographical error "Roger's."

Content/Process: In one sense, this story seems to function as Friedman's comment on the premise of Rogers's "trifle impertinent" opening question. Both this story and that question have as their theme the naive but all-too-human assumption that one who is admirable must be like us in essential ways.

23. BUBER: Now may, may I tell you a story, not about me, eh, but a true eh story, too, eh, not just an anecdote. Eh, eh, a Christian eh, eh officer, officer—I don't— colonel, or so—eh, had to explain eh some people in eh—I think—in Wales, had to explain them something in the war, in the Second War, [unintelligible] to explain them something—soldiers—eh, something about the Jews. Eh, it began, of course, uh, with eh the uh explanation uh what Hitler eh, eh means and so on, eh and he explained to them that eh the Jews

23. Transcription: Previous transcripts have edited this turn extensively to increase readability and presumably to remove ambiguity.

Content/Process: Buber's story reinforces the impact of Friedman's, also focusing on naïveté when an innocent Christian confronts the complex otherness of Jewish culture. Taken together, the stories might be heard as a mild rebuke to Rogers, although the tone of the interchange is one of good humor. (While it is clearly valuable and interesting to speculate on possible meanings and

are not just a barbarous race, they had a great culture and so on; and the, now, then, he addressed a Jewish soldier that was there and knew something and told him, "Now you go on and tell them something." And this eh eh young Jew told them something about eh eh Israel and eh even about Jesus. And eh, to wit, one of the soldiers answered, "Do you mean to tell us that before your Jesus we have not been Christian people?" [Extended laughter] [3.5]

intentions, we consistently reminded ourselves that we have little or no direct access to what Buber, Rogers, and Friedman meant that night in 1957. This, of course, is a hermeneutic caveat that applies to any textual discussion. What we are trying to illustrate here, of course, is a broader set of concerns not always dealing with what the individual principals *intended*, but also with what an audience heard and how the dialogue itself unfolded with a life and voice[s] of its own.]

24. BUBER: Now you go on.

25. ROGERS: Oh no. [unintelligible—not after this?]

26. BUBER: No? [More laughter]

24–26. Transcription: Previous transcripts have deleted turns 24–26, which happened amid laughter. We have treated turn 24 as a separate Buber turn—though adjacent to his previous turn—because of the laughter, the significant pause, and the topic shift.

II

Mutuality and Therapy

27. ROGERS: Well, I'd like to um shift to a question that I have often wondered about. Um, I have wondered whether [3.1] your concept—or your experience—of what you have termed the I-Thou relationship is uh similar to what I see as the effective moment in a therapeutic relationship. And I wonder, uhm—if you would permit me—I might take a moment or two to say what I see [Buber: Yes, yes] as essential in that, and then perhaps you could comment on it from your point of view.

Um, I feel that when uh when I'm being effective as a therapist [Buber: Mmmm], I enter the relationship as a subjective person, not not as a scrutinizer, not as a scientist, and so on. [Buber: Uh] Um, I feel, too, that uh when I am most effective, then somehow I am relatively whole in that relationship, or the word that has meaning to me is [Buber: Uh] is "transparent." That is, there [Buber: Uh] is nothing—um, to be sure there may be many aspects of my life that aren't

27. Transcription: (a) Although Rogers asked of Buber whether "your concept—or your experience—of what you have termed the I-Thou relationship" is similar to effective moments of therapy, previous transcripts have deleted "or your experience." This qualifier, however, is significant for understanding the interaction, because in it Rogers suggests that Buber answer not only conceptually, but that he also stay grounded in his own concrete experience— the realm that Rogers himself intended to emphasize. Buber, of course, saw himself as also grounded in concrete experience (e.g., Buber, 1967, p. 689; Buber, turns 4, 6, 8, 10, 12 above). (b) Previous transcripts have edited Rogers's last sentence of this turn so that it would mirror Buber's use of "meeting."

Content/Process: (a) Rogers begins his question with what could be called an alignment strategy, advertising his familiarity with Buber's work. (b) Rogers specifically

29

brought into the relationship, but what is in the relationship is transparent. There is nothing, nothing hidden. [Buber: Mmm] Um, then I think, too, that in such a relationship I feel a real willingness for this other person to be what he is. I call that "acceptance." I don't know that that's a very good word for it, but my meaning there is that, um, I'm willing for him to possess the feelings he possesses [Buber: Uhm], to hold the attitudes he holds, to be the person he is. [Buber: Mmm] Um, and then I suppose uh another aspect of it that is important to me is um that I think in those moments I really am able to sense with a good deal of clarity the way his experience seems to him, really uh viewing it from within him, and yet without uh losing my own personhood or separateness [Buber: Uh huh] in that. [Buber: Hmm] And, um, then, if if in addition to those things on my part, my client or the person with whom I'm working um is able to sense something of those attitudes in me, then it seems to me there real, is a real, um experiential meeting of persons, in which uh each of us is changed. Um, I don't

stresses that his question applies not to the entire relationship of therapist-client, but only to "the effective moment" of such relations. Thus, he does not claim the prolonged or full mutuality/equality of roles for which Friedman and others have sometimes criticized him: "Must [the therapy relationship] be based on a one-sided inclusion, as Buber holds, or *on full mutuality at every level, as Rogers claims?*" (Friedman, 1965, p. 31, emphasis added).[15] Interestingly, Buber also responds to Rogers's question *as though Rogers has not qualified it* by referring only to an "effective moment." One little-known fact provides historical context for this question. About this time, Rogers was working on a paper (1956a, 1956b, 1959a) that conceptualized the importance of crucial "moments" of therapy— turning points or critical incidents in which the communication is especially involving and from which growth is more likely to come. Throughout the remainder of his career, Rogers maintained his belief that dialogue in therapy is at best a matter of "moments," even to the point of identifying this belief as consistent with

---

15. Actually, Friedman has been somewhat inconsistent in his treatment of this issue. Although he has usually criticized Rogers for arguing inappropriately for a "full," "total," or "complete" mutuality, he has also presented a different view: "Rogers does *not* claim total mutuality. . . . At first glance it appears as if Rogers is talking about total mutuality. *He never is*" (Friedman, 1986, pp. 417–418; also 1994, p. 54). Later in this dialogue, Friedman also provides an interesting comment on this issue (see turn 122).

know—I think sometimes the client is changed more than I am, but I think both of us are changed in that kind of of an experience.

Now, um, [3.4] I see that as having *some* resemblance to the sort of thing you have talked about in the I-Thou relationship. Yet, I suspect there are differences. At any rate, I, I would be interested very much in your uh comments on how that um description seems to you in in relation to uh what you have thought of in terms of two persons moving, or or uh an I-Thou kind of relationship.

Buber. In fact, during the last year of his life, *thirty years after the dialogue*, Rogers replied to another scholar's article with an unmistakable reference to his conversation with Buber. In a lengthy paragraph we need not reproduce here, Rogers mentions the importance of "moments" of dialogue five times and identifies these moments as when Buber's "I-Thou relationship" bonds two people. "At such important moments of change in therapy," he wrote, "the question of [overall] equality or inequality is *totally* irrelevant" (Rogers, 1987, p. 39; emphasis in original). Further: "Since I, as therapist, hope that I have helped this moment to come about, the relationship can be looked upon as an unequal one. But in the moment itself, all such issues disappear" (p. 39).[16] (c) Significantly, Rogers weaves into this utterance (in one form or another) all three of the facilitative conditions he had written about earlier and would flesh out in his later writing. The reference to

---

16. In our view, Buber and Rogers agreed in the dialogue to a far greater extent than other commentators have recognized that therapeutic mutuality occurs during moments (see Anderson & Cissna, 1996a). Although he didn't say so directly in the dialogue, Buber, too, was sensitive to the significance of "moments." Buber's argument about address, response, responsibility, and direction in life recognizes that the call to which one responds (or doesn't) exists in a *moment*—and a most significant one—when a person's life may be reordered. He discusses moments explicitly in *Between Man and Man* (1947/1965a), at one point discussing the "God of a moment, the moment God" addressing the person (p. 15) and at another describing how the response from any address that gives direction to life arises "in moments" (p. 114).

transparency presages congruence, the overt reference to acceptance reflects his interest in "unconditional positive regard," "prizing," and the like, and he includes a clear if indirect reference to empathy in which he mentions the same stipulation of nonfusion that Buber himself consistently stressed (that one's own separate ground must not be lost). (d) The client has to perceive these factors, Rogers said, in order for there to be a "meeting" in which each is changed. He stresses that although the client could be presumed to change more than would a therapist, both are changed by their dialogue. This comment actually restates Buber's notion in turn 4 that Buber feels he does not have "the right to want to change another if I am not open to be changed by him as far as it is legitimate." (e) Rogers finishes his turn by acknowledging that he may not have understood Buber well enough, and by requesting that Buber frame his answer not just in terms of his own concepts, but in relation to Rogers's.

28. BUBER: Now I may try—but eh allow me to ask eh questions, [Rogers: Uh huh] too [Rogers: Uh], about what you mean. First of all, I would say, eh this is the action of a therapist. Its eh a very good example for a certain mode of eh dialogic existence. I mean: Two persons have a certain situation in common. This situation is, from your point of view—point is not a

28. Transcription: (a) Previous transcripts have Buber saying that Rogers described a good example for a "certain moment" of dialogic existence. Actually, he did not repeat Rogers's word here, but said "a certain mode of eh dialogic existence." (Given Buber's accent, he might have said "mood" instead, but "mode" credits Buber with better semantic

good word, eh but let's see it from your point of view—it is a sick man coming to you and asking a particular kind of help. Now, look down [unintelligible—Rogers overlaps]—what would you see?

29. ROGERS: May I interrupt there?

30. BUBER: Yeah, please do.

31. ROGERS: I, I feel that um, if, if, from my point of view, this is a sick person [someone pours water], then probably I'm not going to be of as much help as I might be. [Buber: Mmm] I feel this is a *person*. [Buber: Mmm] Uh, yes, somebody else may call him sick, or if I look at him sort of from an objective point of view, then I might agree, too, "Yes, he's sick." But in entering the relationship [Buber: Mmm], it seems to me if I am looking upon it as, as "I am a relatively well person [Buber: Mmm] and this is a sick person"—

clarity.)[17] (b) Previous transcripts delete the "look down" comment at the end. Although its intent is unclear, Buber may have been trying to express the inherent inequality of therapist and client, and even a condescension that characterizes some therapists.
Content/Process: Although Buber begins by saying he too will ask questions, he then develops neither a question nor a clarification of Rogers's point but rather pursues his own extension of it.

31. Content/Process: Rogers interrupts to stress that a therapist using the word "sick" presumes a kind of response to a client that is unlikely to be helpful. Rogers's point, in context, seems to be that this label itself *presumes* inequality. In a sense, this observation, although subtle, capsulizes much of the philosophical distinctiveness of the respective positions of Rogers and Buber.

---

17. Buber was fluent in nine languages, German, Hebrew, French, English, Polish, Latin, Greek, Yiddish, and Italian (Friedman, 1991a, p. 321), but English was not foremost among them. According to Buber's granddaughter, who grew up in his home, his first foreign languages were French and Italian, and his first public lecture in English did not occur until 1947 (Buber would have been 68 years old). She described him as quite a "showman" and said that when he was in front of an audience "he could perform" regardless of the language (Judith Buber Agassi, personal communication, September 1, 1995). Although Buber was an eloquent speaker of the English language, as illustrated in this dialogue, at times his accent could make him difficult to understand.

32. BUBER: No, but this I don't mean.

33. ROGERS: —no good.

32. Transcription: Other transcripts have "Which I don't believe."

Content/Process: Buber denies that he intends the meaning Rogers interpreted for "sick," and in turn 34 renounces the word in restating the problem. Note that in his first extended turn (#4 above) Buber professed an interest in "man in the *so-called* pathological state," and he said he "doubted . . . if it is the right term."

34. BUBER: I don't mean this. I— let me—let me eh leave out this uh word "sick." [Rogers: Uhm] A man coming to you for help. [Rogers: Uh huh] The difference— the, the essential difference— between your role in this situation and his is obvious. [Rogers: Uh huh] He comes for help to you. [Rogers: Uh huh] You don't come to help for him. [Rogers: Uh huh] And not only this, but you are *able*, more or less, to help him. He can do different things to you, but not just help you. And not this alone. You *see* him, really. I don't mean that you cannot be mistaken [Rogers: Um hmm], you see, but you *see* him, just as you said, *as he is*. He cannot, by far, cannot see *you*. Not only in that degree, but even in that eh *kind* of seeing. Eh, you are, of course, a very important person for him. But not a person whom he wants to see and to know and is able to. You're important for him. You're—he is, eh,

34. Transcription: Previous transcripts have cleaned up the verbal slips in "You don't come to help for him."

Content/Process: (a) Buber asserts—without specific example or evidence—that the client cannot help the therapist. Yet Rogers said in his first question that he and other therapists are indeed personally helped in therapeutic encounters. Buber's comment appears to discount Rogers's experience and claim without referring overtly to them. (b) Buber, in suggesting the inherent inequality of the relation, categorically asserts that the therapist is "not a person whom he [the client] wants to see and to know and is able to." Although Rogers does not contradict Buber's claim in this dialogue, he had ample experiential evidence by this time of many clients wanting to see and know him personally (Kirschenbaum, 1979). (c) If it is true that the client "is not inter-

from the moment he comes to you, he is, eh eh may I say, eh entangled in your life, in your thoughts, in your eh, eh being, eh your communication, and so on. But he is not interested in you as you. It cannot be. You are interested, you say so and you are right, in him as this person. This eh-eh kind of detached presence he cannot have and give. And now this is the first point, as far as I see it. And the second is—now, please, you—

ested in you as you. It cannot be," Rogers may be surprised, based on his knowledge of Buber's writing, at why Buber could say earlier that this is a kind of *dialogic* existence. The Rogers papers in the Library of Congress provide a clearer picture of Rogers's prior familiarity with Buber's work. As early as 1952, a syllabus shows that he taught Buber to his Chicago graduate students, and we found his notes from reading two printings of *I and Thou* (trans. R. G. Smith; published in Edinburgh by T. & T. Clark in 1937 and 1950), a classroom handout based on *Between Man and Man*, and notes from Maurice Friedman's *Martin Buber: The Life of Dialogue* (1955b) (Rogers, nd-c, nd-d, nd-e, nd-f, nd-g). Rogers also included quotations and close paraphrases from Buber's *Between Man and Man* and Friedman's *Martin Buber: The Life of Dialogue* within the questions he prepared for the dialogue. Clearly Rogers sounded surprised at this turn in the conversation; in a halting statement deleted from previous transcripts, he says "I'm not [Buber: Yes] entirely sure—." Rogers responds next with another almost textbook-style perception check. (d) Similarly, by at least December, 1952, Buber was aware of Rogers's work and had expressed to Friedman his interest in it (Buber, 1952b, 1952c). Between early 1953 and 1956, Friedman sent to Buber—or had sent to him—various of Rogers's papers as well as drafts of his own discussion of Rogers from the psychotherapy chapter of his book, *Martin Buber: The Life of Dialogue* (1955b) (Friedman, 1952, 1953, 1955a, 1956).

35. **ROGERS:** [Unintelligible] Uh, yes, I'm not, [Buber: Yes] I'm not [Buber: Yes] entirely sure—

35. **Transcription:** This turn is omitted in the B-F transcript.

36. **BUBER:** You may, you may interrupt me any moment.

36. **Content/Process:** Perhaps responding to a nonverbal cue of Rogers's interest, Buber again invites Rogers to interrupt, providing clear evidence of goodwill and responsiveness in the dialogue.

37. **ROGERS:** Oh, all right. I uh I really wanted to, to understand that. Um, the fact that I am able to see him with less distortion than he sees me [3.1], and that I do have the role of helping him and that he's not uh, uh [Buber: Mmm] trying to know me [Buber: Uh] in that same sense—that's what you mean by this "detached presence"? Uh—

37. **Content/Process:** In his perception check, Rogers explicitly phrases the problem in terms of role and Buber's specific phrase, "detached presence." He carefully stipulates that the role difference is that the therapist sees with less distortion, that the therapist tries to help the other, and that the client does not try to know the therapist "in that same sense." Buber agrees in turn 42 that "Yes, only this" was what he meant. From Rogers's perspective, none of these points evidently contradict his perception that therapy has moments of dialogue in which therapist and client do understand each other in some senses, if not in the "same sense," and in which *both* therapist and client are helped.

38. BUBER: Yes, h-mmm hmm.

39. ROGERS: I just wanted to make sure I—

40. BUBER: H-hmm. Hmmm.

41. ROGERS: OK.

42. BUBER: Yes [Rogers: Okay], yes, only this.

43. ROGERS: Uh huh.

38, 40, 43. Transcription: These turns are omitted in other transcripts.

41, 42. Transcription: These turns are reversed in other transcripts.

44. BUBER: Now, the second fact, as far as I see as a fact, is in this situation that you have in common with him, only from two sides. You are on one side of the situation on the, may I say so, eh, more or less active, and he in a more or less patient, not entirely active, not entirely passive, of course—but relatively. And, this situation—let us now look on this common situation from your point of view and from his point of view. The same situation. [Rogers: Uh] You can see it, feel it, experience it from the two sides. From his side, for—oh, let's begin—from your side seeing him, eh, eh observing him, eh knowing him, eh helping him—but he—from your side and from his side. [Rogers: Uh huh] You can experience, eh, I would eh venture to say, bodily, experience his side of the situation. When you *do*, so to speak, something to him, you *feel* yourself *touched* by what you do to him. [Rogers: Uh huh] He cannot do it at all. You are at

44. Transcription: (a) Buber said: "When you *do*, so to speak, something to him, you *feel* yourself *touched* by what you do to him." Previous transcripts have not noted the inflections, and have inserted the word "first" after "touched." (b) The B-F transcript changes one point of Buber's slightly, having him say: "And this, you will, you not only will, you want, your inner necessities may be sure as you are." Buber's actual comment, midway through the turn, though ungrammatical, makes more sense to us as it does not attribute consciousness to "inner necessities."

Content/Process: (a) In this turn, Buber strongly asserts his claim to be certain about the therapeutic relation; he assumes he can even refer to Rogers's own experience with certainty ("certainly in your experience as a therapist . . . you must experience it again and again"). (b) Despite Rogers's attempts at inclusion with clients

your side and at his side at the same time. Here and there, or let's rather say, there and here. Where he is and where you are. He cannot be but where he is. And this [2.8], you will, eh, not only you will, you want. Your inner necessity may be as they are. I accept that. I have no objection at all. But the situation has an objection. Eh, you are—you have—necessarily another attitude to the situation than he has. You are able to do something that he's not able. You are not equals and cannot be. [Rogers: Hmm] You have a great task—self-imposed—a great self-imposed task to *supplement* this need of his and to do rather more than in the normal situation. But, eh, of course, there are limits, and I may be allowed to tell you—certainly in your experience as a therapist, as a healing person or helping to healing, eh you must experience it again and again— these limits to [2.8] simple humanity. You—"to simple humanity" meaning: Being, I and my partner, so to speak, alike to one another, on the same plane. I see, you *mean* being on the same plane, but you cannot be. There is not only you, your, your, eh, eh mode of thinking, your mode of eh eh doing, there is also a certain situation— things are so and so—which may sometimes be tragic and even eh more terrible than what we call tragic. You cannot change this. [Buber sighs] Humanity, human will, human understanding, are not everything. There is some reality

(Buber: "You are at your side and at his side at the same time") and his desire for mutuality, Buber claims that "the situation has an objection." Presumably the client's situation imposes limits on his (or her) ability to be on the same "plane." Buber's point is clear and reasonable, but his metaphor of a situation itself "objecting" is surprising in that "situations" are discussed as if they possessed independent expressive existence and potency. (c) In this turn, it becomes clear that Buber equates "equality" to similar role-dependent attitudes in an overall situation; if there are different roles and interpersonal limits placed on persons, they cannot be "equal." To Rogers, however, equality cannot be determined in this way—equality is achieved in moments of mutual recognition of basic personness, even if the parties have dissimilar role limitations (Rogers, 1951, 1961, 1980). Note that Buber here has forgotten about or decided not to respond (yet) to Rogers's point about "moments."

we confront [Rogers: Uh huh]—is confronting us. [Rogers: Uh huh] We cannot—we may not—forget it for a moment. [2.7]

45. ROGERS: Well, what you've said certainly stirs up lots of reactions in me. Uh, one of them, I think, is this. [2.7] That uh—let, let me begin first on a point that I think we would agree on. [Buber: Uhm huh] I suspect that, that um, uh you would agree, too, that if this client comes to the point where he can experience what he is expressing, but also can experience my understanding of it and reaction to it, and so on, then really therapy is just about over.

45. Content/Process: (a) Rogers attempts to rephrase the issue in terms of therapeutic progress: If the client can achieve what Buber would call being on one side and the other at the same time, then therapy would be successful. In discussing the limits of mutuality in psychotherapy, Buber makes precisely the same point. In his famous postscript to *I and Thou*, written only months after his dialogue with Rogers, Buber wrote: "But again the specific 'healing' relation would come to an end the moment the patient thought of, and succeeded in, practising 'inclusion' and experiencing the event from the doctor's pole as well" (1958, p. 133). (b) To this point, Rogers has asked questions of Buber, facilitated their talk, and clarified his understanding of Buber. In this turn and the next, Rogers asserts that he can also respond to Buber by presenting his own position and even by disagreeing mildly.

46. BUBER: Yes. This is just what I mean.

46. Transcription: The CR transcript reports that Buber, responding to Rogers's turn 45, said "Yes. This is *not* what I mean" (emphasis added). The B-F transcript attempts to solidify that statement by adding the word "but": "Yes. *But* this is not what I mean" (emphasis added). *In fact, the tape verifies that Buber intended something quite different.* He says to Rogers, "Yes. This is *just* what I mean" (emphasis added); and, as we noted immediately above, Buber's 1958 postscript to *I and Thou* contains a virtual paraphrase of the point on which Rogers thought they would surely agree. This different statement is a significant change not because it turns Buber's point 180 degrees (it really does not), but because it puts Rogers's *next* comment in a different light. Instead of seeming to dismiss Buber's disagreement, he is actually building on Buber's agreement. This is one of those transcriber errors that go unquestioned in the literature simply because so few people can or do recheck the original recording. Such errors are not so rare—as we found many others in the transcripts of this conversation.

47. ROGERS: Okay. But the, the other, one other thing that I feel is this. I've, I've sometimes wondered whether this is simply a personal idiosyncrasy of mine, but it seems to me that uh when another person is, is really expressing himself and his experience and so on, um, I don't feel, in the way that you've described, different from him. That is—I don't know quite how to put this—but I feel as though [3.8] in that moment his way of looking at his experience, distorted though it might be, um,

47. Content/Process: Rogers specifies how his own attitude as therapist is based on offering the other a sense of equality in one crucial way: however "distorted . . . it might be," the effective therapist experiences a client's perception as having "equal authority, equal validity" with his own interpretations. He is careful to repeat the key word "equal." Characteristically, Rogers sees this kind of equality as the "basis of helping." Also characteristically, Rogers is careful to state here that the kind

is something I can look upon as as having equal authority, equal validity with the way I see life and experience. And it seems to me that that really is is the basis of helping, in a sense.

48. BUBER: Yes.

49. ROGERS: And I do feel that's a real sense of equality between us.

50. BUBER: No doubt of it. But eh I am not speaking now about your feeling but about a real situation. I mean, you two look, as you just said [Rogers: Uhm huh], on *his* experience. Neither you nor he look on *your* experience. The subject is *exclusively* he and his experience. He cannot in the course of, eh let's say, a talk with you, he cannot change his position and eh, eh ask you, "Oh, Doctor, eh where have you been yesterday? [Rogers: Uh huh.] [Laughter] Eh, oh, have you been eh the movies? [Rogers: Uh huh] What was it and how were you impressed?" [Rogers: Uh huh] He *cannot* do it. [Rogers: Uh huh] So, eh, I, I see and feel very well your feeling, your attitude, your taking part. But you cannot change the given situation. There is something objectively real that confronts you. Not only he confronts you, the person, but just the situation. You cannot change it.

of equality to which he refers does not depend on the difference of objective roles, which is obvious, but to the two parties' granting each other's perceptions equal authority (in this sense, an "authorness," or the ability to legitimize what is "real"). Rogers believed that people aren't helped by experts telling them answers to their problems, but by therapists and clients building a relation of mutual listening on equal *experiential* footing, even if not on fully equal *role* footing.

50. Transcription: In this turn, we are confronted with the problem of transcribing homophones. In context, it makes more sense that Buber would have meant "you *two* [therapist and client together] look . . . on his experience," rather than (as in other transcripts) "you *too* [also] look . . ." Not only was Buber just introducing his point, but he continues his argument in the next sentence referring specifically to the therapist and client.
Content/Process: Buber has just agreed with, or at least acknowledged, Rogers's point about equal perceptual authority being the basis of helping, and he clearly agrees that Rogers is correct in feeling there is a "real sense of equality" between therapist and client. His next statements, however, seem to admonish Rogers by discounting "feeling" as the basis of equality in favor of a criterion of

"real situation." Buber seems to point to role distinctions when he uses "real situation"—the situation of therapy in which the client is unable to escape personal self-consuming troubles, although the therapist has better perspective. Buber categorically asserts that "Neither you nor he look on *your* experience. The subject is *exclusively* he and his experience." Rogers does not contradict Buber here, perhaps deferring to his assigned role as facilitator-interviewer for this dialogue. Yet he has just told Buber that his clients *are* indeed often aware of Rogers's experience (turn 27). Buber has again either overlooked or dismissed Rogers's personal observations. Interestingly, too, Buber said "neither you nor he"—yet he might have recognized that in the condition of "congruence" (summarized in turn 27), Rogers explicitly included being aware of and sensitive to his own experience. Rogers argues that, to a certain extent, both he and his client are aware of the experiencings of self and the other (although clients are not likely to be as aware as Rogers is). Buber's comment contradicts Rogers boldly not only about the experience of the client, but his statement that "neither he nor you look on *your* experience" strikes at the core of client-centered theory regarding therapist congruence. That is, effective therapists *are* aware of, and "look at," their own experiences in therapy.

Perhaps this explains why, in his next turn, Rogers asks if he can clarify who is Martin Buber.

51. ROGERS: Well now, now I'm wondering uh who is Martin Buber, you or me, because what I feel—

52. BUBER: Heh, heh, heh. [audience joins laughter]

53. ROGERS: —because—

51–52. Transcription: The B-F transcript removes any notation of audience laughter at this point.

Content/Process: Rogers's wondering who is Martin Buber could be, we speculate, a lighthearted way of disagreeing. Without overstating the issue, and leaning toward humor in bringing it up, Rogers perhaps is implying that he feels closer to the spirit of Buber's concept of dialogue, at least as he previously understood it, than was Buber at this time and on this issue. Rogers seems surprised at Buber's vehemence in denying the felt experience of therapist and client as Rogers reports it.[18] From Rogers's perspective, how can therapy be dialogical if *neither* therapist nor client take into account (include) the therapist's experience (Buber: "neither he nor you look on *your* experience")?

54. BUBER: I'm, I'm not, I'm not, eh, so to say, "Martin Buber" eh, as, how do you say, with uh-uh the signs, brackets? Yes—no?[19]

54–56. Transcription: Much of this interchange is changed or omitted in previous transcripts. For example, Buber never says: "I'm not, so to say, 'Martin Buber'

---

18. Years later in discussing the dialogue during his oral history interviews with David Russell, Rogers said as much himself: "I thought Buber's ideas of the I-Thou relationship was [sic] a very good description of the best moments in therapy. I was surprised to find he didn't think that" (Rogers & Russell, 1991, p. 143).

19. Several suggestions are offered apparently from the platform: "brackets," "parentheses" (twice—once Rogers?), then something unintelligible, a

55. ROGERS: In that sense, I'm not "Carl Rogers" [Buber: I'm not—] either. [Laughter]

56. BUBER: Yes, you see, I'm not a quoted man that eh thinks so and so and so on.

as, how do you say, with quotes," despite this statement being attributed to him. Buber was fishing for the right word, and several possible words were suggested; "quotes" was evidently suggested from the audience, though none of this is noted in other transcripts.

Content/Process: This is the only time in the dialogue that the audience assumes a vocally active role. The informal atmosphere established on the stage and the closeness they felt with Buber led, as it might in everyday conversation, to their supplying a word that the other was hunting for.

57. ROGERS: I know.

57. Transcription: Existing transcripts have Rogers replying "I know. I realize that," although the last three words were never said. These transcripts also merge Rogers's turns 57 and 59.

58. BUBER: We were just speaking about [Rogers: Sure] eh, eh something that interests us, perhaps, in the same [Rogers: Right] measure. You're in another kind, you are always eh, eh in eh contact with, in practical contact with—

58. Transcription: This turn is omitted from previous transcripts. However, it is important in showing how Buber was also willing to serve a facilitative role to get things back on track. Despite a number of episodes in which Buber appears to assume primarily an expert-respondent role, at this moment, he is also interested in facilitation (for other examples, see turns 24 and 26).

"Hmm," another "parentheses" (Friedman?), then someone yells, apparently from the audience, "quotes."

59. ROGERS: Now, let's forget that facetious remark. What, what I wanted to say is this: Uh, that I think you're quite right, that there is an objective situation there [Buber: Uh huh], uh one that could be measured, one that is real [someone pours water], one that various people could agree upon if they examined the situation closely. But um it has been my experience that that is reality when it is viewed from the outside, and that that really has *nothing* to do with the relationship that produces therapy. [Buber: Umm] That is something um [2.5] immediate, equal, a meeting of two persons on an equal basis— even though, even though in the world of [Buber sighs] I-It, that could be seen as a very unequal relationship.

59. Transcription: (a) For some reason, Rogers's "Now, let's forget . . ." has been changed in previous transcripts to "Aside from . . ." The differences are subtle, but real. (b) Previous transcripts delete, here and elsewhere, virtually all the vocalized encouragements and affirmations the speakers provided each other. This decision diminishes for readers the sense of good-will and mutual agreement between them, even when there were real disagreements.

Content/Process: (a) The implication of this statement is that Rogers agrees that if the "objective situation" is analyzed, then things could be seen as unequal—certainly the power relations and knowledge bases within the situation are unequally distributed. If the relation is scrutinized externally and analytically, then it appears unequal. Yet experientially, in good therapy as Rogers defined and observed it, the two parties sense their equal validity as persons. (b) In turn 54, Buber may have been attempting to head off Rogers reciting Buber's own published work to him, preferring for Rogers to engage the live Buber on stage with him. He was unsuccessful, as we see at the end of this turn, and perhaps his sigh anticipated the reference he thought Rogers was about to make to Buber's published ideas.

60. BUBER: Hmm. Now, Dr. Rogers, this is the first point where we must say to one another, "We disagree."

61. ROGERS: Okay. [Laughter]

60. Content/Process: This statement is further indication why Buber would not have said (or meant) in turn 46, "This is not what I mean" as previous transcripts indicate, because turn 60 then would not be the "first point" where they would have said to one another that they disagreed.

62. BUBER: Eh, you see, I [5.7] I cannot only look on you, on your part of things, of your expon-, experience. [Rogers: Uh huh] Let me say, if—eh, let's take the case that I could talk to him, to your patient, too. I would, of course, hear from him eh a very different tale about this *same* moment. [Rogers: Yes] Now, you see, I am not a therapist. I'm interested in you *and* in him. [Rogers: Uhm huh] I *must* see the situation. I must see you and him in this dialogue hampered by tragedy. [2.6] Uh, sometime, in many cases, a tragedy that can be overcome. Just in your method. I have eh no objection at all to your method, you see? Eh, there is no need to speak about it. [Rogers: Uh huh] Eh, but sometime eh method is not enough, and it cannot do what has been—what is—necessary to do. Now, let me ask you a question that I, uh, seemingly has nothing to do with this [Rogers: Uh huh], but eh it's the same point. Eh, you have certainly much to do with schizophrenics. Is it true?

62. Transcription: (a) Two words clearly stressed by Buber (same, must) were not emphasized in previous transcripts, while one word (him) was transcribed with a stress we did not hear. (b) In a significant change, existing transcripts have Buber saying, "I must see you and him in this dialogue bounded by tragedy"; however, he actually said that he saw therapist and client in dialogue "hampered by tragedy." Tragedy, rather than bounding dialogue, hampers it. (c) Instead of "method is not enough. You cannot do what is necessary to do," we heard Buber say: "method is not enough, and it cannot do what has been—what is—necessary to do." (d) Rather than "Is it so?," Buber said "Is it true?"
Content/Process: Although they have seemingly just agreed to disagree, with Rogers's "Okay," Buber continues to try to persuade. Evidently he considers this a crucial conceptual point, one that Rogers has not yet understood. Given Rogers's experience and theory of therapy, however, he might have wondered too if his

own point was being understood by Buber. Buber said: "Eh, you see, I I cannot only look on you, on your part of things, of your expon- experience. . . . Let's take the case that I could talk to him, to your patient, too. I would, of course, hear from him eh a very different tale about this *same* moment. Now, you see, I am not a therapist. I'm interested in you *and* in him. I *must* see the situation." Buber seems to state this as a contrast to what he perceives as Rogers's lim- ited perspective in therapy, but Buber's point sounds virtually identical to what Rogers would describe as the dialogue of therapy. Rogers has already said that the therapist must practice inclusion, too, becoming interested in self *and* other. Rogers believes *he* "sees the situation," too. Buber continues to press his point, fram- ing it in terms of Rogers's "method" and saying he has no objection to the method. Framing the issue in terms of your conver- sation partner's "method" while counterposing your own ability to "see the situation" that is more "real" could be a way of trumping Rogers's point. Rogers, again per- haps recognizing his facilitative role, does not comment.

63. ROGERS: Some. Uhm huh.

64. BUBER: You have, have you, also, to do, let me say, with para- noiacs?

63–67. Transcription: At the end of turn 62, Buber asks if Rogers had dealt with schizophrenics, and follows up by asking about his experience with paranoiacs. To each question, Rogers responds

65. ROGERS: Some.

66. BUBER: Hum?

67. ROGERS: Some.

that he has indeed had "some" experience. Previous transcripts delete even more indication that Rogers had indeed dealt with such clients: In turn 63, Rogers said "Some" but his next "uhm huh" for emphasis was omitted; furthermore, in turns 66 and 67, deleted in other transcripts, Buber even checks his hearing and Rogers repeats "some."

Content/Process: As we pointed out in another study (Cissna & Anderson, 1994, p. 41), this corrected interchange is significant for one interpretation of Buber's theory. Friedman (1983), evidently arguing that Buber was correct about the inability of a client to understand a therapist's experience, wrote that "Buber asked Rogers whether he had ever worked with schizophrenics and paranoiacs and was not surprised when Rogers answered in the negative" (p. 226). In other words, Friedman recalled that Rogers had not worked with these especially challenging clients. Yet he had, and said so in the dialogue. Further, in a paper he delivered just ten months later at a symposium on psychotherapy with schizophrenics Rogers makes clear that his clinical experience with schizophrenics has been extensive (Rogers, 1958b). Presumably, too, the invitation for him to speak at this conference was made as a result of mental health researchers recognizing his previous therapy with schizophrenics. This paper also illustrates Rogers's emphasis on "moments" of relation and empathy (p. 7) rather than full mutuality. Late in the paper, Rogers states that "Still another meaning would be that the effectiveness of therapy lies in an immediate relationship [here CR inserts, handwritten with a carat, 'an existential encounter *now*,'] not in an understanding of past experience. This would run counter to much current therapeutic thinking"˙ (p. 18). Although Buber was not cited, the reference to "existential encounter" may indicate he was thinking of Buber. Interestingly, how Buber phrased his question in the dialogue—"You have certainly much to do with schizophrenics. Is it true?"—does not indicate an expectation that Rogers hadn't conducted therapy with schizophrenics, as Friedman suggested, but, of course, the opposite. Two further points are intriguing, if less central to our interpretation. First, when Rogers reminisced late in his life about the dialogue (Rogers & Russell, 1991), he mentioned that he learned at breakfast with Buber the next morning that Buber's psychiatric coursework dated to the turn of the century (as Buber essentially said in the dialogue—turn 4). Because schizophrenia was then understood as "real damage to the brain" (p. 201), Rogers thought this might have accounted for Buber's difficulty in understanding how Rogers could have a relatively "equalitarian relationship with someone who was so damaged" (p. 201). We note also, however, that Buber had just come from lecturing at the Washington School of Psychiatry, founded by Harry Stack Sullivan, which was distinguished precisely, as Leslie Farber, chairman of the faculty of the school put it in a letter to Buber, by its "continuing concern with the treatment of schizophrenia" (Farber, 1991). If Buber's formal coursework was long ago, surely his knowledge of psychiatry in general and of schizophrenia in particular was far more current. Second, in the fall of 1957, Rogers left the University of Chicago for a joint appointment in psychology and psychiatry at the University of Wisconsin, for the express purpose of pursuing research on psychotherapy with schizophrenics (see Rogers, 1967). Rogers's experience with schizophrenics at Wisconsin led him to revise his theory slightly, giving more emphasis to the need for therapist congruence or genuineness and allowing positive regard to become somewhat conditional, as Rogers and his client-centered colleagues often found it necessary with severely schizophrenic clients to initiate the relationship if any was going to be established (Rogers, 1966, pp. 186, 189–190; Rogers & Stevens, 1967, pp. 99–100, 181–192; cf. Thorne, 1992, pp. 83–84).

68. BUBER: Now, would you say that the situation is the same in the one case and in the other? Meaning, the situation as far as it has to do with this relationship between you and the other man. Is this relationship that you describe the same kind of relationship in the one case and in the other? Can you talk eh—this is a case with, eh, eh a question, that interests me very much [Rogers: Uh huh], because I was interest very much by paranoia in my youth. Eh, I know much more about eh schizophrenia [Rogers: Uh huh], but I often am much impressed and I would want, uh like to know, have you—this would be, mean very much—eh, can you eh meet the paranoiac just in the same kind? [3.1]

69. ROGERS: Let me first qualify my answer to some degree. Uhm, I haven't worked in a psychiatric hospital. My my dealings have been with people for the most part who are able to at least make some kind of an adjustment in the community, so that I don't see the really chronically—

70. BUBER: Oh, I see.

68. Transcription: Buber's comment that he often was "much impressed and I would want, uh like to know, have you—this would be, mean very much—eh, can you eh meet the paranoiac just in the same kind?" has been changed in existing transcripts to "very much interested, and I would like to know, have you—this would mean very much—can you meet the paranoiac just in the same kind?" Obviously, because "impressed" and "interested" are not synonyms, and Buber did not say "very" before "impressed" (or "interested"), some external interpretations were being added here.

Content/Process: (a) Buber's comment that he knows much more about schizophrenia should be considered in the context of Rogers's later discovery (see Rogers & Russell, 1991) that at least some of Buber's factual knowledge was, by 1957 standards of psychiatric research, dated. (b) Buber's sincere invitation to hear more of Rogers's experience—and how much it would mean to him—is noteworthy here because it contrasts somewhat with his conversational style in the dialogue, which may have sounded lecturish to Rogers. The invitation triggers some expansiveness in Rogers's subsequent responses, including qualifications to his initial answer.

70. Transcription: Previous transcripts delete Buber's further acknowledgment that Rogers had in fact worked with schizophrenics and paranoiacs.

71. ROGERS: —ill people. [MB: Uh huh] On the other hand, uh, we do deal with individuals that, who are both schizophrenic and others who certainly are paranoid. And—uh [3.7]—one of the things that that I say very tentatively, because I realize this is opposed by a great weight of psychiatric and psychological opinion, uh, but I would say that there is *no* difference in the relationship that I form [Buber: Hmm] with a normal person, a schizophrenic, a paranoid [Buber: Hum]—I don't really feel any difference. [Buber: Hmm hmm] That doesn't mean, of course, that when—well, again it's this question of looking at it from the outside. Looking at it from the outside, one can easily discern plenty of—

71. Transcription: (a) "Certainly are" has been transposed in previous transcripts. (b) Rogers strongly emphasizes that there is "*no* difference" in the relationships he forms with schizophrenics and paranoiacs on one hand and normal persons on the other; this emphasis is omitted in previous transcripts, as have been Buber's audible recognitions that he hears Rogers.

Content/Process: As Buber points out, Rogers *does* consistently phrase observations not in terms of underlying unities or theories, nor in particularly conceptual terms, but by referring to his own "feelings." Because of this rhetorical habit, his statements sound less forceful and theoretically justifiable than Buber's—and perhaps more easily dismissed.

72. BUBER: No, no—I don't mean—

72. Transcription: This turn was omitted from previous transcripts, which blend Rogers's turns 71 and 73 as one long statement. Perhaps Buber here is attempting to soften the tone of the disagreement developing between them.

73. ROGERS: —differences. I don't either. And, and, it seems to me that, um, that if therapy is effective, there is this *same kind of meeting of persons* no matter what the psychiatric label.

And and one minor point in relation to something you said

73. Transcription: (a) Previous transcripts delete Rogers's "I don't either" response to Buber's interjection, and change his "and" to a "but," thereby altering his comment subtly. (b) Previous transcripts also diminish the force with which Rogers asserts that the

that, that struck me. It seems to me that um [2.8] the moments where, where persons are most likely to change, or I even think of it as the moments in which people *do* change, um are the moments in which perhaps the relationship is experienced the same on *both* sides. When you said you might talk to my patient and you would get [Buber: Uh] a very different picture, I agree—that would be true in regard to a great many of the things that went on in the interviews. But I [Buber: Huh] suspect that in those moments [Buber: Uh huh] when, um, when real change occurred [Buber: Uh huh], that it would be because there *had* been a real meeting of persons in which um it was experienced the same from both sides.

meeting between therapist and schizophrenic is similar to the therapist–"normal person" relation. Rogers strongly inflects "same kind of meeting of persons," although other transcripts fail to note this. (c) Existing transcripts inexplicably replace "you might talk" with "if you talked," and "suspect" with "should expect."

Content/Process: Again, Rogers emphasizes not that the relationship of therapy is one of full equality, but that in certain critical *moments* where change is likely, the relationship may be experienced as essentially the same by both parties. Although he labels this point as "minor," he has in fact foregrounded it before and—we could infer—considered it a notable difference from Buber's external view of the "real situation" (in which role differences and differences of expertise are predominant). Rogers wanted to depict the relationship as felt from the inside.

74. BUBER: Uh huh. Yes. This is, this is really important. Eh—

74. Content/Process: Probably, Buber's "yes" is one of recognizing Rogers's point here, not necessarily one of agreement.

75. FRIEDMAN: Can I interpose a uh [Buber begins to talk] question here? As—

76. BUBER: No. Would you, would you wait a moment? [Friedman: All right, thanks but—] I only want to explain to Dr. Rogers

75–76. Transcription: (a) Just as Buber begins to talk about his "really important" point, Friedman speaks. The B-F transcript deletes this interruption, along with Buber's objection to it and Friedman's background reply, "All right, thanks but—." The CR and

why this question is particularly important [Rogers: Uh huh] to me and your answer, too. [Buber sighs]

I, eh [4.5], a very important point in my thinking is the problem of limits [3.3], eh, meaning, I do something, I try something, I will something, and in—I give all my thoughts, eh, all my existence—*into* this [Uh huh] eh doing. And then I come, at a certain moment, to a wall [Rogers: Hum], to a boundary, to a limit that I *cannot*, I cannot ignore. Eh, this is true, also, for what interests me eh more than anything: human eh effect of dialogue. That by, meaning by dialogue not just talking. Eh, dialogue can be eh silent. You could, we could, perhaps, eh, not, eh without the audience. I would eh recommend to do it without an audience. Eh, it's, eh, we could eh, eh sit together, or rather walk together [Rogers: Uh huh] eh in silence [Rogers: Uh huh] and that eh could be a dialogue. [Rogers: Uh huh] That eh—so, so even in dialogue, full dialogue, there is a limit set. [Rogers: Uh huh] This is why I'm interested in paranoia. There is—eh—here is a limit set for dialogue. I can—it is sometimes very difficult to talk to a schizophrenic. He, in certain moments—as far as *my* experience with this, of course, with, of it, eh [3.2 with Buber sigh] how may I say, a dilettante? [Rogers: Uh huh]—eh, I uh can talk eh to a schizophrenic as far as he is willing to let me in in his

P transcripts retain most of the interchange. (b) As he does throughout the evening, Rogers respects several of Buber's long pauses without interrupting, pauses that are not noted in existing transcripts. Meaningfully—although perhaps only coincidentally—Buber chooses just this place in the conversation to affirm that dialogue does not involve "just talking" ("just a talking" in previous transcripts), but also "dialogue can be eh silent." This is another example of how the conceptual issues of Buber and Rogers can be understood most profitably in the context of their talk; *content* (what they discuss) and *process* (how they discuss it) are intertwined. (c) The B-F transcript substitutes "terrifyingly" for "terribly," and also inserts "I feel this terrible fate very strongly" instead of what Buber actually said, "And eh this, the terribility of this fate, eh, I'm feeling very strongly. . . ." (presumably to avoid the awkward "terribility," although Buber's meaning was clear enough). (d) Buber says that what interests him "more than anything" is the "human eh effect of dialogue," rather than "human effective dialogue," as other transcripts report it.

Content/Process: (a) Buber seems curt in deflecting Friedman's interruption, perhaps demonstrating the intensity of his listening to Rogers's point. (b) Buber recognizes that an audience (such as the one present that evening) is not a neutral addition to an interper-

particular uh world [Rogers: Uh huh] uh that he, that is *his* own; and that in general he does not want to eh have you come in, or other people. But he lets some people in. Eh, and so he may let me in, too. But if, in the moment when he shuts himself, I cannot go on. And the same, only eh in a terrible, terribly, eh, eh strong eh manner, is the case with paranoiacs. He, he, uh he does not open himself and does not shut himself. He *is* shut. There is something eh else eh being done to him that *shuts him*. And eh this, the terribility of this fate, eh, I'm feeling very strongly because in the world of *normal* men, there are just analogous eh cases [Rogers: Uh huh], when a sane man behaves, not to everyone, but behaves to uh some people *just so*, eh being shut. And the problem is if if he can eh, eh be opened, if he can open himself, and so on. [Buber sighs] And this is a problem for uh humans in general.

sonal conversation, but an active set of influences limiting and/or encouraging the flow of the conversation in many ways. He describes this as an example of the more general necessity to recognize limits to social dialogue. Those human relations practitioners who believe that dialogic philosophy proffers only gentle humanistic sharing should consider how Buber was concerned with the practical and difficult limits placed on human communication. (c) In a particularly revealing turn, Buber demonstrates how certain he is of his conclusions. Although Rogers has said that he's had experience treating schizophrenics and Buber has had no such experience (in fact, labeling himself a "dilettante"), Buber continues to assert he is right when they disagree.

77. ROGERS: Yes, I think I see that as, as—

78. BUBER: Yes, now, Dr. Friedman may want to come—

77–78. Transcription: This interchange was quite different than what was reported in previous transcripts. The CR and P transcripts change some wording, and the B-F transcript deletes the entire interruption. Friedman (as editor) undoubtedly believed, we think appropriately, that this and other interruptions reduced somewhat the readability of the dialogue.

Content/Process: Scholars of dialogue will also be interested in the attitudes of the participants toward each other and in how they managed their talk, especially as this dialogue's agreed on topic was dialogue itself. After his own extended speech, Buber interrupts Rogers's attempt to reply, and instead calls on Friedman to bring up an issue that may be—for all he knows—an abrupt topic change. We have suggested (Cissna & Anderson, 1994) that Buber's conversational rhetoric here surprisingly tended to emphasize certainty over provisionality. This is an instance in which it appears that Buber thought his statement could stand without reply as the last word on a topic. We have previously called this Buber's "rhetoric of cannot," which appears similar to what Edwards referred to as Buber's "tendency to resolve difficulties by verbal fiats" (1970, p. 79). Conversation analysts use the term "current speaker selects next" to describe how turns are allocated by a speaker who overtly nominates the next speaker (see Nofsinger, 1991, pp. 82–83 for a simplified explanation). The power of this move in an ostensibly two-person dialogue is an interesting phenomenon; a speaker interrupting a dialogue partner by calling on a third participant, in this case a moderator, effectively forecloses discussion on a particular idea. Although what this suggests about Buber's approach to dialogue is not altogether encouraging, his action could also be interpreted in the context of his desire to acknowledge Friedman's earlier attempt to enter the conversation—a laudable motive. (b) Buber's interruption also functioned to ratify Friedman as a participant—not just a functionary—in the dialogue. Buber believed that dialogue required the opportunity for full participation by all parties, and he may have been attempting to protect Friedman's right as a moderator to clarify and question. Had Buber not called on Friedman here, surely Rogers would have replied directly to Buber; and had Friedman thereby not been given this opportunity to enter the dialogue, perhaps he would not have participated as fully as he did in the second half of the dialogue. Interestingly, this might not have bothered Rogers. Years later Friedman (1987, pp. 392–393; 1994, p. 47) reported that he sensed that Rogers was "annoyed" and "irritated" with him for "getting in the middle of his dialogue with Buber" (these are Friedman's words, not Rogers's), a suspicion he confirmed later through a mutual friend. Perhaps this incident, where Rogers was interrupted in order to give Friedman the floor, stimulated that annoyance.[20]

---

20. Papers from the Rogers collection at the Library of Congress suggest that Rogers may not have understood fully the roles he and Friedman were to assume that evening. Among Rogers's materials connected with the dialogue were two short pages that appear to be notes for introducing Buber. They include a brief chronology of Buber's life and a few lines summarizing some of Buber's major ideas and sources of influence. They include the unattributed line, from Rogers a powerful compliment, which seems to be

79. FRIEDMAN: In, uh—this is my role as moderator. Um [Buber: Hum], I'm not—the only role I play here—uh, I'm not quite satisfied as to whether uh [Buber: Huh] in this interchange, just before the paranoiac-schizophrenic, um to what extent it's an issue, to what extent it *may* be a different use of terms, so let me uh ask Dr. Rogers one step further. As I understood what Buber said was that the relationship is an I-Thou one, but not a fully reciprocal one, in the sense that while you have the meeting, nonetheless you see from his standpoint and he cannot see from yours. And in your response to that, you you pointed again and again to the meeting that takes place and even to the change that may take place on both sides. But I didn't hear you ever point to, to suggesting that he does see from your standpoint, or that it is fully

79. Transcription: (a) Although the CR and P transcripts mistakenly report that Friedman said, "I didn't hear you even point to . . . ," Friedman's own B-F transcript restores the correct word, "ever." This indicates that Friedman might have checked the transcript and edited some things for accuracy, not just readability. The rest of the same sentence, however, was not corrected. Among other differences, the P transcript inserts one "not" that was never said, while the B-F transcript inserts two "nots" never said ("does not see" and "is not fully reciprocated"). The need for editing, of course, is clear; Friedman's original question, as Rogers actually heard it, was probably ambiguous to Rogers. (b) Previous transcripts do not include a 4.5 second pause at the end of Friedman's turn, followed by laughter—perhaps trig-

---

in quotation marks, that "his person does not give the lie to his works" (Rogers, nd-a). Hence, Rogers may not have realized that a moderator would be present, who, among other duties, would introduce both Buber and himself, and who would also be able to interject himself directly into the dialogue. Friedman also supports this interpretation. In a handwritten note at the end of a letter written only five days after the dialogue in which he invited Rogers to be one of a number of scholars to participate in a "philosophical interrogation" of Buber planned for the *Review of Metaphysics*, Friedman provides an account to Rogers for his own role in the dialogue: "Neither Martin Buber nor I had understood adequately the way you, and no doubt Ross Snyder too, had conceived the dialogue. If we had, we probably would not have thought a moderator necessary or desirable" (Friedman, 1957). (Rogers said that the dialogue was "set up by Ross Snyder" [Rogers & Russell, 1991, p. 201]. That and other clues lead us to believe that Snyder first suggested the event and may have functioned as a liaison between Rogers and the Michigan people.)

reciprocal uh in the sense that he also is, is helping you. And I wondered if this might not be uh perhaps just a difference, if not of, of words, of viewpoint, where you were thinking of how you feel *toward* him, that is, that he is an equal person and you respect him. [4.5 second pause—then laughter]

gered by someone's nonverbal behavior on stage.

Content/Process: (a) Friedman makes a sincere, if unsuccessful, effort to clarify Rogers's view; unfortunately, Buber responds instead of Rogers. (b) In contrast to the premise of Friedman's question, we interpret Rogers's previous statements as indeed suggesting that the client *can* sometimes see from the standpoint of a therapist's experience (see turns 27, 83), though of course not exactly, and Rogers had suggested that the client *does* sometimes help him (see turns 3, 34). Rogers might be forgiven here if he felt somewhat misunderstood and mischaracterized.

80. BUBER: There remains a *decisive* difference. It's not a question of objecting helping the other. It's a question of *wanting* to help the other. He is a man wanting to help the other. [Rogers: Yes] And he, his whole attitude is this eh active, helping attitude. This is [Rogers: Hhm]—I had, I used to say, totality of different, eh by the whole heaven, but I would rather prefer to say by the whole *hell*— difference from your eh attitude. [Rogers: Uh huh] This is a man in hell. [Rogers: Uh huh] A man in hell cannot think, cannot imagine eh helping another. How *could* he?

80. Transcription: (a) A confusing and essentially meaningless sentence in previous transcripts ("It's one thing to help the other.") is clarified by listening to the tape itself. Buber's actual statement makes good sense in this context: "It's a question of *wanting* to help the other." (b) Another reported Buber statement that makes little or no sense also resulted from transcription errors. Existing transcripts have: "There is . . . a difference by the whole heaven, but I would rather prefer to say by the whole *hell*, a difference from your attitude. This is a man in *health* [actually, "hell"]. A man *helped* [actually, "in hell"] cannot think, cannot imagine helping another." Buber would not have identified a man in hell as a healthy man. It is surprising that scholars have not double-checked this obviously nonsensical utterance previously, but instead evidently accepted it literally.

Content/Process: (a) After Buber called on Friedman and Friedman addressed his question explicitly to Rogers, *Buber* answers—leaving Rogers to reply both to the question and to Buber's forceful extension of it. Any hope Rogers might have had of responding to Buber's previous point (from turn 76, before Friedman's turn—on how inherently "shut" a client may be) has now vanished. (b) Buber apparently believes that differences in experience between a knowledgeable helper and a frustrated helpee in a kind of "hell" create an existential gulf across which the client cannot imagine traveling.

81. ROGERS: But that's uh [3.3] that's where—that is where some of the difference arises. Because it seems to me, again, that in uh in the most real moments of therapy [2.6] I don't believe that this intention to help [2.7] is any more than a substratum on my part either. In other words, surely I wouldn't be doing this work if that wasn't part of my intention. And when I first see the client, that's what I hope I will be able to do, is to be able to help him. And yet in the, in the interchange of the moment, I don't think my mind is filled with the thought of "Now I want to help you." It is much more, um, "I

81. Transcription: Rogers pauses often in this turn—again, unnoted in previous transcripts—and Buber respects each pause.

Content/Process: (a) Buber's previous turn (#80) is perhaps his most animated and passionate of the evening. Following it, Rogers is more subdued and perhaps deferential, pausing more often than in any utterance to this point. (b) Rogers once more emphasizes that he is characterizing only the "most real moments of therapy," "the interchange of the moment," and is not describing the whole therapeutic relationship. Both Buber's and Friedman's comments

want to understand you. What what person are you behind this paranoid screen, or behind all these [Buber: Eh] schizophrenic confusions, or behind all these masks that you're wearing in real life?" [Buber: Huh, uh huh] "Uh, who are you?" And um, I don't feel that, that uh—it seems to me that that *is* a desire to meet a person, not, not, "Now I want to to help." It seems to me that it is more that um: I've learned through my experience that when we *can* meet, then help does occur, but that's a by-product.

seem to refer globally to the relationship or to its enduring objective conditions. Unfortunately, Rogers, the expert on listening, does not highlight this difference forcefully. (c) In a significant extension of his theory of therapy, Rogers replies to Buber's point by assuring him that a therapist who emphasizes "helping" as a goal or plan paradoxically may not be very helpful. (His notion may be heard as analogous to his earlier objection to Buber's use of the word "sick.") Rogers's point is also consistent with his later claim (1966; Rogers & Stevens, 1967, pp. 186–187) that the therapist, whatever his or her guiding theories, must attempt to experience the relation with each client *atheoretically* at the time of meeting (a notion certainly similar to Buber's requirement of surprise in dialogue). The effective therapist renounces the attitude of "Now I want to help you" in favor of "Now I want to understand you." This insight is at the core of his life's work. Help should not be the overriding goal of therapy, he clarifies in this comment, but a "by-product" of an effective relationship characterized by *moments* of relative equality.

82. FRIEDMAN: Dr. Rogers, would you not agree, though, that this is not fully reciprocal in the sense that that man does not have that attitude toward *you:* "I want to understand you. What sort of a person are you?"

82. Content/Process: Friedman persists and now is able to get a direct response from Rogers. Friedman asks, in effect, a leading and somewhat argumentative question—one that structures and presumes its own answer. Friedman, however, clearly wants to relate his inquiry as much to what Rogers didn't say as to what he did; the leading question was his vehicle for doing so.

83. ROGERS: That's, that's um, um—the only modification I made of that was that perhaps in the moments where real change takes place, then I wonder if it isn't reciprocal in the sense that uh [3.0] I am able to see this individual as he is in that moment [Buber: Uh huh] and he really senses my understanding and acceptance of him. And that I think is what *is* reciprocal and is perhaps what produces change. [3.0]

83. Content/Process: Again, we hear Rogers's emphasis on the "moments" of real change rather than a totalizing concern with an ongoing state of full mutuality or equality. It almost seems that he believes that if he repeats this word often enough, then Buber and Friedman will recognize his point. (Rogers in one of his other roles—as an educator of young therapists trying to learn empathic styles— would know better.) Rogers's statement is relatively unfocused— and hardly a strongly worded reply to Friedman. He could have made more explicit that he was talking only about occasional moments. His reply does, however, reassert that at least some kind of mutual recognition and mutual experience exists in these moments of therapy. At another level, it also suggests— in the words of Friedman's question—that the client does want to "understand" at least this portion of a therapist's experience, and that the client in these moments definitely adopts an attitude of curiosity that could be characterized by "What sort of person are you?"

84. BUBER: [Sighs—audience laughter] Hmmm. You see, I, eh, of course, am entirely with you as far as your experience goes. I *cannot*

84. Transcription: Previous transcripts do not note the long pause, the very noticeable sigh from Buber, or the audience laughter.

be with you as far as I have to look on the whole situation, your experience and his. You see, *you* give him something in order to make him equal to you. You *supplement* his need in his relation to you. You *make* him uh—of a certain—may I say so personally, out of a certain fullness you give him what he wants in order to be *able* to be, just, just for this moment, so to speak, on the same eh plane with you. But even that is eh [2.8]—very—it is a tangent. It is a tangent that may not last but one moment. It is not the situation, as far as I see, not the situation of an hour; it is a situation of minutes. And these *minutes* are made possible by you. Not at all by him.

Content/Process: (a) Buber again implies that Rogers as a therapist seems locked in his own experience and unable to see the "whole situation" as Buber is able to see it. In this turn we hear an important example of what could be termed the fragmentary character of Buber's listening. Buber here concedes that a kind of equality is possible—but that it is made possible by the therapist (that is, the client alone could not will it), and it is not possible for a matter of hours, but of "minutes." Buber says that the equality Rogers describes "may not last but one moment." "*Moments*," of course, were what Rogers was stressing throughout. Buber's statement has the *tone* of refuting Rogers's point, even while its *content* supports virtually the same notion Rogers advanced. The basis of therapy is that the relationship is legitimized ("made possible," in Buber's words) by the therapist at first in order to establish moments of equality from which the client grows. Buber's final sentences of the turn, of course, reflect precisely how Rogers would characterize the situation—despite the role differences, therapists can make possible moments of equality (see, e.g., Rogers, 1956a, 1956b, 1959a). (b) Perhaps there is more agreement than Buber, or even Rogers, was willing to acknowledge. Rogers never claimed total equality, and at this point in the dialogue Buber recognized that for brief moments, made possible by the therapist, therapist and client are on the same plane (see Anderson & Cissna, 1996a). (c) In his statement, "as far as I see," Buber reflects some of the same style of provisionality as does his partner. They may be accommodating their views somewhat to each other, and here we see how each man also seemed to take on something of the conversational style of the other as the dialogue progressed.

85. ROGERS: Uh huh. Although, although, I do sense a—that last I would thoroughly agree with—but I do sense some some real disagreement there because um it seems to me that, that what I give him [2.3] is permission to be. [2.9] [Buber: Hmm. Heh heh] Which is not—which is a little different somehow from bestowing something on him, or something like that.

85. Content/Process: (a) Rogers notes the essence of Buber's agreement, but chooses to frame it as him (Rogers) agreeing with Buber, rather than the other way around. He does not point out that his partner might have misunderstood him earlier, nor does he attempt to score debaters' points with the audience. All this is consistent with Rogers's and Buber's roles enfolded in the dramatic presentation that was their dialogue that night. He highlights only one subtle point of metaphor. He doesn't think he "bestows" something tangible as a therapist (Buber had used "give" and "supplement" to suggest that something was transferred to the client), but grants a kind of "permission to be." (b) The word "permission," used by Rogers in turn 85 and by Buber in turn 86, actually echoes Rogers's opening question (turn 3) where he talks about a "therapeutic relationship that gives us permission, almost *formal* permission, to enter into a deep and close relationship with a person." (c) Interestingly, an article in *Science*, reporting on a program at the American Psychological Association convention that honored Rogers on the occasion of his 75th birthday, used the phrase "permission to be" in its title ("Carl Rogers," 1977).

86. BUBER: I think no human being can give more than this. [3.1] Making eh life possible for the other, if only for a moment. [3.3] Permission.

86. Transcription: (a) One of the most obvious transcription errors of the dialogue occurs in this turn. Buber does not say "I'm with you," as existing transcripts report, but "Permission." Both statements are positive, yet the difference is important. Buber reflects Rogers's term "permission," which is one marker of effective listening. (b) Previous transcripts do not note the two extended pauses only seconds apart. Both exceed three seconds, the length of silence conversation analysts (see McLaughlin, 1984, pp. 115–116) believe constitutes a "conversational lapse" that usually becomes awkward for participants if it occurs at a transitional point within a conversation (which this obviously is). Buber may be trying to yield the floor to Rogers, but for some reason Rogers does not take it. Note that after each silence, Buber increases his alignment with Rogers; starting with a genuine compliment, he enriches it by referring again to "moments" and uses Rogers's term, "permission."

87. ROGERS: Well, if we don't look out, we'll agree. [Laughter]

87. Content/Process: Rogers, perhaps conscious of his facilitation role, emphasizes agreement instead of disagreement, even while ironically recognizing their previous disagreement.

88. BUBER: Now let's go [unintelligible: on?].

88. Content/Process: Buber's task-related comment, less characteristic of him in this dialogue, sounds abrupt—almost like a professor who is redirecting class discussion.

III

Inner Meeting and
Problems of Terminology

89. ROGERS: Uh, I really would like to shift this to another topic [Buber: Hmm] um, because [2.9], if as I understand [Buber overlaps: Huh] what you've written and so on, it seems to me that I discern one other type of meeting which has a lot of significance to me in my work that, as far as I know, um, you haven't talked about. Now I may be mistaken on that, I don't know. And what I mean by that is that it seems to me one of the most important types of meeting or relationships [Buber: Hmm] is the person's relationship to himself. [Buber: H-hmm] In in, uh, therapy, again, which I have to draw on because that's my background [Buber: Sure] of experience—

90. BUBER: Of course.

91. ROGERS: —um, there are some very vivid moments in which the individual is meeting

89–90. Transcription: (a) The B-F transcript deletes "Now I may be mistaken on that, I don't know. And what I mean by that is that ...." The P transcript omits from this section only "by that." (b) All previous transcripts delete Buber's clearly audible insertion, "Sure," when Rogers explains again that he must draw on therapeutic experiences because they are his professional background. (c) Rogers's reference to the necessity to draw on his background in psychotherapy probably reflects his discovery just prior to the dialogue that Buber's sponsors told him "not to speak with Rogers about psychotherapy" (Pentony, 1987, p. 420). Rogers didn't know what else they could discuss meaningfully, and resolved that, regardless, there was nothing "to stop him from speaking about psychotherapy to Buber" (p. 420). Obviously, Buber ignored the advice. (d) Turn 90 was also deleted in previous transcripts.

uh some aspect of himself, a feeling he has never recognized before, uh, something of a meaning in himself that he has never known before, and where—um. It could be any kind of thing. It may be his intense feeling of aloneness, or uh the terrible hurt he has felt [Buber: Hmm], or or something quite positive [Buber: Hmm] like his courage, and so on. Um, but at any rate, in those moments, it seems to me that um there is something that partakes of the same quality that I understand in a real, real meeting relationship. That the— he is in his feeling and the feeling is in him. It is something that uh suffuses him. He has never experienced it before. In a very real sense, I think it could be described as a real meeting with an aspect of himself that he has never met before. Now I don't know whether that um um seems to you like um uh stretching the concept you've used. I suppose I just would [Buber: Hum] like to get your reaction to it. Whether, whether to you *that* seems like a possible type of of real relationship or a "meeting"? Because, well, I guess I I'll push this one step further. That I guess I have the feeling [2.6] that it is when the person has met himself in that sense, probably in a in a good many different aspects, that then and perhaps only then, is he really capable of meeting another in an, in an I-Thou relationship.

Content/Process: Rogers here clearly shifts the conversation to different ground. In doing so, he takes a risk because he now has reason, given Buber's previous comments, to believe that his partner will disagree with his characterization of a person's inner meeting or "relationship to himself." This may help explain why Rogers's introduction to this issue is more halting and somewhat less fluent than many of his other statements, even though this was one of the nine questions Rogers had prepared in advance.

92. BUBER: [Buber sighs] Now here eh we approach eh a problem of language. [Rogers: Uh hum] You call something eh dialogue [Rogers overlaps: Um hum] that I cannot call so. [Rogers: Um hum] But I can explain why I cannot call it so, why I would want another term between dialogue and monologue for this. Now, for what I call dialogue, eh, there is essentially necessary the moment of surprise. Eh, I mean—

93. ROGERS: [overlaps] Moment of surprise?

92. Content/Process: (a) Buber is reminded of a specific "problem of language" in Rogers's statement, and, curiously, says that Rogers has "call[ed] something eh dialogue that I cannot call so." He indicates the need for a different term than "dialogue" for the phenomenon Rogers mentioned. Yet Rogers did *not* say "dialogue" in his description or question, but "meeting." In fact, in this brief turn, Rogers refers to "meeting" seven times. Buber evidently assumed that Rogers had said—or meant?—dialogue. This may be an instance of Buber mishearing Rogers, or he may have presumed a meaning beyond the words. Apparently, the issue of dialogue with the self was discussed at the seminars Buber had conducted recently at the Washington School of Psychiatry (Friedman, 1983, p. 257), and perhaps Buber was sensitized to this topic. Conceivably, Rogers did mean to refer to dialogue generally (several turns later, he is more explicit on this), but it is hard to assume that "dialogue" was the intent of this particular question, considering his persistent and careful avoidance of the term in favor of another of Buber's concepts. (b) "You call something eh dialogue that I cannot call so" from this interchange has been cited (Arnett, 1981) to suggest Buber's general disapproval of Rogers's overall understanding of dialogue. Taken in context, it is clear this was not Buber's intent, although Buber may justifiably have believed that Rogers's views on dialogue (and other scholars' as well) were less sophisticated than his own. (c) Buber's response is somewhat disappointing because, although his objection to using the term "dialogue" to discuss an inner meeting is very clear, we never find out what Buber thinks about the *phenomenon* or what, if anything, he would call it. Hycner (1991) describes the question, "Can one have a dialogue with one's self?," which is perhaps the question Buber thought Rogers had asked, as the most frequently asked question by those who are not familiar with Buber's concepts. Hycner's answer is that one cannot, because dialogue "requires two persons entering into a genuine relationship with each other" (p. 51). Hycner, however, goes on to tell us what he does call this process—an "intrapsychic dialectic," referring to the interaction between two polarities within a single person. (d) Friedman, in writing about Buber's struggles to write his autobiography, provided an interesting comment on Buber's objection to internal dialogue: "In the seminars at the Washington School and in his dialogue with Rogers, Buber steadfastly objected to speaking of a 'dialogue with oneself' because it lacks the otherness and surprise necessary for real dialogue. But in this case [he is discussing Buber's autobiographical writing] at least, one can speak of 'A Dialogue of Self and Soul,' to use the title of a poem by Yeats!" (1983, pp. 257–258).

94. BUBER: Yes eh, being surprised. [Rogers: Um huh] Eh, a dialogue—let's take a huh rather eh eh trivial image. The dialogue is like a game of chess. Eh, the whole eh charm of eh the g- eh of chess is that I do *not* know and cannot know what my partner will do. I'm surprised by what he does and on this surprise eh the whole play is based. Now, you hint at this, that a man can surprise himself. [Rogers: Uh huh] But in a very different manner from what from how a person can surprise another person. Eh—[21]

94. Content/Process: (a) Buber emphasizes surprise as a basic element of dialogue. This is certainly consistent with Rogers's assurance in his question that clients "meet" portions of their experience that they've never met before, much like they could meet strangers. Thus, Rogers is speaking metaphorically. Buber's suggested countermetaphor, chess, is indeed an interpersonal one, and he asserts that inner meeting is "very different" from interpersonal surprise. We do not know if or how Buber elaborated on this distinction; from the transcript we discover little about why Buber thought Rogers's metaphor inadequate compared with his own. (Many players, by the way, would qualify Buber's characterization of the charm of chess. Surprise is an element, of course, but if it happens too often, one is surely losing. Far from finding it impossible to anticipate— "do not know and cannot know" —what a chess partner will do, a thoughtful player, although never

---

21. Apparently no tape recording was made for a short period at this point. The tape resumes in Rogers's turn below. All transcripts, including Rogers's original typescript, provide this identical explanation: "While the tape was being changed, Dr. Buber went on with his description of the characteristics of a true dialogue. A second feature is that in true meeting, or dialogue, that which is different in the other person, his otherness, is prized."

absolutely certain, is able to construct a relatively precise calculus of the other's alternatives, along with one's own.) In sum, Buber's metaphor seems no closer to the spirit of his philosophy of dialogue than does Rogers's metaphor. (b) Buber later addressed this question in an essay, "The Word that is Spoken," which was first published in 1961—and in language that sounds very much like a response to Rogers. He noted that the "so-called dialogue with oneself" is "possible only because of the basic fact of men's speaking with each other; it is the 'internalization' of this capacity" (Buber, 1965b, p. 112). He called it "thinking" and "speaking the inner word" (pp. 112–113) and then referred precisely to the two qualities he had argued to Rogers were absent in inner dialogue. Buber wrote: "the ontological presupposition of conversation is missing from it, the *otherness*, or more concretely, the *moment of surprise*" (p. 113, emphasis added).

95. ROGERS: I think that um your—the first two aspects of that, um—I, I hope that perhaps sometime I could play some recordings of interviews for you to indicate how the *surprise* element really can be there. That is, a person can uh be expressing something and then suddenly be hit by the meaning of that which has come from someplace in him that he doesn't recognize. In other words, he

95. Transcription: (a) Previous transcripts alter Rogers's turn in a variety of ways, most of them to aid readability. The major substantive change removes any indication of the forcefulness of Rogers's statement. He places strong vocal emphasis on "surprise" in the first sentence, and on "definitely" in the fifth: "That can *definitely* happen." This is Rogers's strongest expression of certainty in the dia-

really is surprised by himself. That that can *definitely* happen.

Um, but the element that I see as being most foreign to your concept of dialogue is that it is quite true that this otherness in himself is not something to be prized. [Buber: Hmm] I, I think there—in in this kind of dialogue I'm talking about, within—that it is that otherness that probably would be broken down. And and I do realize this probably is, in part, a—uh, the whole discussion of this may be based on a difference in our use of words, too. I mean that uh—

logue. (b) Previous transcripts have not included Rogers's final fragmented sentence that was interrupted by Buber.

Content/Process: (a) This is one of the turns in which Rogers does not defer much to Buber; instead he strongly asserts the importance of his own clinical experience by offering empirical evidence in the form of recordings. Buber probably did not know at this time that Rogers was the first psychotherapist to record and analyze his client sessions systematically (and to publish transcripts of them— see Rogers, 1942a, 1942b), and Rogers evidently believes that his experiences and observations with clients should at least be considered as counterevidence to Buber's metaphorical dismissal of his position. (b) Rogers admits that in this inner meeting the client wouldn't initially "prize" this "otherness," but suggests that at the moment of surprise or insight, that inability would be transcended, or in his term, "broken down." This is why therapeutic dialogue must be defined, Rogers argues, in terms of moments rather than in terms of global or ongoing situations.

96. BUBER: And you see, may I add a *technical* matter? [Rogers: Uh hmm] Eh, I'm I have learned in the course of my life to appreciate terms. [Rogers: Uh hum] Eh, when, eh—and I think that modern psychology, eh does it not in sufficient measure. Eh, when I eh

96. Transcription: Many differences of transcription, some quite meaningful, mark this turn. (a) Buber did not say "a certain mode of the psyche," as existing transcripts have it, but: "a certain mode of the psychic." (b) Buber said "*scream* of the *soul*" rather than, as

find something that is essentially different from another thing, I want a new term. [Rogers: Uh hum] Eh, I want a new *concept*. [Rogers: Uhm huh] Eh, you see, eh, for instance, um modern psychology, in general, eh says about the unconscious that it is a certain mode of the psychic. It has no sense at all for me. If something is so different from one—if two things are so different from one another as this eh *scream* of the *soul*, changing in every moment, where I cannot grasp anything, eh, when I try to grasp it's uh away, eh from one side—eh, this uh being in pure time, and this uh what we call the unconscious, that is not a phenomenon at all. We cannot— we have no access to it at all, we, we have only to deal with its eh effect and so on. We we cannot say this is psychic and this is psychic, the unconscious is something in which eh, eh psychic and eh phys-physiologic eh are, eh, eh, eh how may I say, "mixed?"; it's, it's not enough. Eh, eh they penetrate one another in such a manner that eh, eh we see in relation to this eh the eh terms eh "body" and "soul" are, so to speak, late terms [Rogers laughs], late concepts—and consciousness a primal eh reality. Now, how can we comprehend this eh one concept, right there? Eh, but this is only—eh—

existing transcripts have it, "strain of the soul." (c) Although previous transcripts report "where I cannot grasp anything when I try to grasp its way from one side," Buber actually made better sense: "where I cannot grasp anything, eh, when I try to grasp it's uh away, eh from one side. . . ." (d) Existing transcripts insert "and over against this" after "pure time," even though Buber did not utter this phrase. (e) Buber said "We we cannot say this is psychic and this is psychic" and, presumably to clarify, prior transcripts have inserted "first" and "second" in this sentence. (f) The B-F transcript substitutes the implied referent "the unconscious" for "this" in the comment: "Eh, eh they penetrate one another in such a manner that eh, eh we see in relation to this. . . ." (g) Previous transcripts report that Buber said "concepts are never reality"; however, on the tape he clearly says something quite different. He appears to be finishing his observation about body and soul by declaring "consciousness a primal eh reality." (h) Previous transcripts delete all the words after "concept" in the last sentence.

Content/Process: (a) Buber's first words appear to be a simple topic shift after the previous topic had been exhausted. However, because existing transcripts do not include Rogers's sentence fragment in turn 95, they obscure the fact that Buber interrupted Rogers's attempt to amplify his own position. This utterance turns out to be less a topic shift than a reaction to Rogers's observation that the two may be misunderstanding each other somewhat because of semantic problems. (b) Although no one could read his mind, Buber's critique of "modern psychology"—that it fails to appreciate precise terms and concepts—easily could be interpreted as a thinly veiled criticism of Rogers himself. Rogers is the only psychologist on stage, Buber does not exempt him from the generalization (although he does refer to modern psychology "in general"), Rogers has just said they may be using terms differently, and they have just disagreed about what to call the phenomenon of inner meeting. Buber's comment then turns to a critique of the unconscious, a psychoanalytic concept with which Rogers as a mature therapist had never identified. By invoking such an example, Buber in effect ignores or overlooks Rogers's approach to therapy. The problem of the unconscious, and the conceptual difficulties it caused, were ones Buber had been working on, and was an important subject of his lectures and seminars earlier in his visit to the Washington School of Psychiatry (see Friedman, 1983, pp. 206–210). (c) Buber seems ready to expand his point even further when Rogers interrupts.

IV

Human Nature as Positive or Polar

97. ROGERS: I, I agree with you very much on that, but I think the uh—when when an experience is definitely of a different sort, then it does deserve a different term. I think we agree on that.

Perhaps, since I see time is going by, I'd like to raise one other question that uh has a great deal of meaning to me, and I don't know how to put it. Um, I think perhaps it's something like this: As I see um people coming together *in* relationship in therapy, uh [2.5] I think that one of the things I have come to believe and feel and experience is that um what I think of as as human nature or basic human nature—that's poor, a poor term, you may have a better way of putting it—is something that is really to be trusted. Uhm. [Buber: Hmm] That, uh, and it seems to me in some of your writings I catch that, something of that same feeling. But, at any rate, um, it's been very much my experience in therapy that [Buber: Hmm] um [Buber: Hmmhmm] one does not

97. Transcription: (a) Existing transcripts omit all indications that Rogers now interrupted Buber, perhaps because he thought Buber's comments only tangentially related to the last topic (and not relevant to his own thought at all) and because, as he said, he saw that "time is going by" and he wanted to ask "one other question" before exceeding the time expectation. (b) The B-F transcript deletes Rogers's statement showing concern for the audience, "Perhaps, since I see time is going by. . . ." This statement also seems motivated by Rogers's role, as the time announced and reserved for the dialogue was now about up. (c) Existing transcripts attribute to Rogers language he did not use, although the implications for meaning are minimal: No "quite" was said before "how to put it," and Rogers said "I think perhaps it's something like this" instead of "Let me express it something like this." However benign they may be, such inaccuracies ultimately

need to supply motivation toward the, toward the positive or toward the constructive. [Buber: Hmm] That exists in the individual. [Buber: Hmm] Uh, in other words, that uh if we can release what is most basic in the individual, that it *will* be constructive. Now, I don't know. Again, I just uh hope that perhaps [Buber: Yes] that would stir some comments from you.

undermine a reader's confidence in the genuineness of written transcripts, and should be corrected. (d) The B-F transcript deletes Rogers's last two sentences inviting Buber's response.

Content/Process: (a) When Rogers refers to the inadequacy of his term "human nature" and invites his partner to come up with a better one, he may be alluding to Buber's earlier critique in the dialogue about psychology's lack of concern for correct terminology. Rogers's comment could even be heard as mild sarcasm. (b) What he describes for Buber is a version of his concept of the "actualizing tendency," the belief that persons who are not unduly constrained or ignorant of behavioral alternatives will tend to make not "evil" or destructive choices, but relationally and personally growthful ones (see Rogers, 1961, chaps. 6, 8, and 9, esp. pp. 194–195). Developing this notion in the years before the dialogue, Rogers had been contrasting it with the entrenched positions of psychoanalytic theory (which he thought presented humans as fundamentally deficient or evil) and behavioristic psychology (which to him characterized humans as primarily conditionable input-output systems, little more than packages of behaviors).

98. BUBER: I don't yet see the exact question in this.

98. Transcription and **Content/ Process:** (a) This turn is deleted in the B-F transcript, collapsing two of Rogers's turns into one. Buber's uncertainty or confusion about the question is eliminated and it sounds as if Rogers has asked an overly long and somewhat repetitive question. (b) Buber's comment in turn 98 could mean one or more of several things, including (1) he was genuinely confused by what Rogers was suggesting that he respond to; (2) he wanted a bit more time to formulate his response (analysts of the dialogue sometimes neglect to note that although Buber was an accomplished speaker of many languages, English was far from his most fluent language); or (3) that he wanted to encourage the dialogue to be more in a question-and-answer format (consistent with their enfolded roles) and he perceived Rogers drifting more toward an elaborated sharing of his own positions. Elsewhere (Cissna & Anderson, 1996) we speculate that part of Buber's interpersonal style is based on a "European professor" model in which teaching is done through a dialogue in which students prepare questions on the basis of the teacher's previous comments. Although Rogers's early questions more or less conformed to this model, at least in their initial asking, this one did involve more position-taking. Still, it is a relatively common interviewing style in Europe and North America for questioners to eschew formal questions for brief statements of positions that invite reply or correction from the interviewee.

99. ROGERS: The only question that I'm raising is: "Do you agree?," I suppose. [Buber: Uh huh] Hum. Or, or if I'm not clear, please ask me other questions. I'll try to put it, um, perhaps, in another way. Well, this, this would be a, a contrasting way. [Buber: Hmm] It seems to me that, um [3.3], much of the point of view of orthodox psychoanalysis at least, has um [2.7] held the point of view that when the individual is revealed, I mean when you really get down to what is within the person [Buber: Uh huh], um, that consists mostly of instincts and attitudes and so on [Buber: Hmm] which must be controlled. [Buber: Uh hmm] Um, now, that runs *diametrically* contrary to my own experience [Buber: Uh hmm] that, that, uh which is that when you get to what is deepest in the individual, that's the very aspect that can most be trusted to be constructive or to tend toward socialization or toward uh the development of better interpersonal relationships and so on. Does that [Buber: Uh huh, uh huh] have any meaning to you?

99. Transcription: (a) The B-F transcript deletes the first two sentences, while other previous transcripts also delete additional statements, including the seemingly important point about Rogers recognizing that his restatement of the idea is framed in a "contrasting way." (b) Existing transcripts overlook Rogers's dramatic vocal inflection emphasizing that it's "*diametrically* contrary to my own experience" that the individual's psychological forces must be controlled.

Content/Process: (a) Rogers first takes Buber very literally by phrasing a grammatical question. After a pause and no response from Buber, Rogers says that Buber can ask a question of him in order to achieve clarity. When Buber still doesn't respond, Rogers rather creatively asks the same question but in a very different way. (b) By asking his question through contrasting his position with orthodox psychoanalysis, perhaps Rogers saw an opportunity to clarify—whether for Buber or for the audience—his own rejection of psychoanalytic concepts (in response to Buber's turn 96, which seemed to associate Rogers with the "unconscious" and by extension with psychoanalytic thinking). (c) Rogers's comment about orthodox psychoanalysis and the individual may be an early preview of, and perhaps a stimulus for, Buber's use of "individual" in his final utterance of the evening (turn 126 below). (d) Rogers here clarifies that the actualizing tendency is not toward more self-ishness, but toward socialization, and toward more satisfying relationships with others. This transcript provides one of the clearest responses to those of Rogers's critics who suggest that his philosophy promoted self-absorption. However, too few Rogers scholars have investigated this dialogue for conceptual insight into Rogerian theory (important exceptions are Thorne, 1992; Van Balen, 1990). (e) We note that Rogers this time ends by constructing an "exact question," complying with Buber's implicit request in turn 98.

100. BUBER: I see. [2.5] I would put it in a somewhat different manner. [4.2] As far as I see, when I have to do with, eh, now let me say a problematic person, or just a sick person, a problematic person, a person that eh, eh people call, or want to call, a "bad" person. [Rogers: Uh huh, uh huh] Uh, you see, eh, in general, eh [3.3], the men who have really to do with what we call the spirit are called not to the good people, but just to the bad people, to the problematic, to the eh, to the inaccessible, and so on. Eh, the good people, we can be friends with with them, but

100. Transcription: (a) Previous transcripts again fail to note the long pauses, here and in succeeding turns. We infer from our repeated listening to the tape that Buber (and maybe also Rogers) was becoming noticeably tired by this point in the dialogue. Perhaps ideas were not flowing as readily as they had earlier; it had, in fact, been a long day for Buber at the conference.[22] (b) For some reason, existing transcripts have changed the readily understandable plural form ("the men who have really to do") to singular ("the man who has really to do"). (c) Buber did not

---

22. He gave lectures at the conference at 8:00 p.m. the previous day and that morning at 10:00 a.m., which also included questions ("Program," 1957). It was now nearing 10:00 p.m., almost twelve hours since his lecture that morning.

they don't—uh, obviously—they they don't *need* this. [Rogers: Uh] Eh, I, so, I, I'm interested just in eh the so-called bad, problematic, and so on. And I—my experience is [2.6] if I succeed to—and this is near to what you say, but somewhat different [Rogers: Uh huh]— if I come near to the reality of this person, I eh experience it as a *polar* reality.

say "unacceptable" here, as previous transcripts have it and which makes little sense in this context, but "inaccessible." This changes the interpretation of succeeding turns, which explore Rogers's concept of "acceptance" in relation to Buber's "confirmation." Did they begin this discussion on the basis of a claim by Buber that the problematic, so-called "bad" people are somehow *unacceptable*? No; the transcripts have misled readers. Buber is merely reasserting his notion that some people, by virtue of their own problems, have become, in his word, "shut"—that is, inaccessible. (d) The meaning of another sentence in this turn has been completely changed by previous transcriptions, although there are few conceptual implications. Buber, in saying that "we" (presumably healthy and balanced persons) can be friendly with so-called "good people" but "they don't *need* this," has been misheard as "The good people, they can be friends with them [presumably, the problematic people], but they [referent unclear] don't need them." In other words, the issue of who is friendly with whom, and for what reason, has been revised from clarity to confusion, and Buber is ill-served in the process. **Content/Process:** (a) Clearly, Buber's terms "good" and "bad" refer to the social or implied social stigmas, labels, and attributions for people, not to his own judgments of them. (b) Interestingly,

Buber identifies his position as "near to what" Rogers said, "but somewhat different." Despite this, some commentators (most recently, see Friedman, 1992, 1994, pp. 60–65; Kron & Friedman, 1994) have discussed this difference in their ideas as if it were a stark contrast. Friedman (1994), in considering Rogers's comments on actualization, wrote: "Rogers clearly accepted Buber's I-Thou relationship and made it his own without plumbing the depths of the philosophical anthropology that in his later years Buber judged to be its necessary underpinning" (p. 64). Buber's comment about being "near" to Rogers may simply show his conciliatory and gracious side when he is actually feeling strong disagreement—or, in fact, it may show that Buber himself saw only a relatively minor distinction between his view of "polar reality" and Rogers's basic trust that persons, if able, will seek constructive relations. In his lecture "Elements of the Interhuman," which Buber delivered at the conference the previous evening, Buber's position seems to support *both* Rogers's hopefulness and his own notion that human nature can be polar: "I have never known a young person who seemed to me hopelessly bad. . . . Man as man can be redeemed" (Buber, 1957b, p. 4). When published, "hopelessly bad" became "irretrievably bad" (Buber, 1957a, p. 108, 1965b, p. 78).

101. ROGERS: As a what? A polar?

101. Transcription: This clarification is omitted from existing transcripts.

102. BUBER: Polar reality. [Rogers: Uhm huh.] You see, in general we say this is either A or Non-A. It cannot be A and Non-A at the same time. [Rogers: Uh huh] It can't. It can't. I mean, um, what you say may be *trusted*. I would say this stands in polar relation relation to what can be *least* trusted in this man. You cannot say, and perhaps I differ from you on this point, you cannot say, "Oh, I detect in him just what can be trusted." I would say now when I de-, I see him, I grasp him, eh b-more broadly and more deeply than before, I see his whole polarity and then I see how the worst in him and the best in him are dependent on one another, attached to one another. And I can help—may be able to help—him just by helping him to change the [2.6] relation between the poles. Eh, not just by choice [Rogers: Uh huh], but by [3.2 with Buber sighing] a certain [4.3] strength that he gives to the one pole in the relation to the other, they being qualitatively very alike to one another. I eh would say eh [8.8] there is not as we generally think eh in the soul of a man good and evil opposed. There are—eh, there is again and again in different manners a polarity, and the poles are not good and evil, but rather [4.2] yes and no, rather eh acceptance

102. Transcription: (a) Previous transcripts insert "in" in the eighth sentence, "when" in the ninth, and "I" in the tenth, for sense. (b) The silences in Buber's speech, unnoted in previous transcripts, become more noticeable than in earlier turns—evidence, perhaps, that Buber is growing weary. For example, in this turn, Buber pauses once for almost nine seconds, nearly an interminable time in a flowing conversation, and almost three times the length of the linguists' usual three second definition of "conversational lapse." Rogers, Friedman, and the audience stay with him.
Content/Process: Buber claims that "You cannot say, and perhaps I differ from you on this point, you cannot say, 'Oh, I detect in him just what can be trusted.'" He remains unsure ("perhaps I differ") about how distant Rogers's point might be from his own, but he draws a distinction based on his polar reality (direction-aimlessness, yes-no, acceptance-refusal) compared to what he sees as Rogers's focus only on trust in human goodness. We note, however, that Rogers did not say he *only* perceived or *only* (or simply) trusted goodness—he did not claim, in Buber's words, "Oh, I detect in him [the other] just [only?] what can be trusted." We interpret Rogers's phrasing as his way of saying that human nature is funda-

and eh refusal. [Rogers: Uh uhm] And we can strength-, we can strengthen, we can help *him* strengthen, the one positive [Rogers: Uh hmm] pole. [Rogers: Uh hmm] And even, perhaps, we can strengthen the force of direction in him because this polarity is very oft, uh often directionless. It is a chaotic eh state. We could bring in a cosmic note into it. Eh, we can help put order, eh, put a shape into this. Eh, because I think the good, or what we may call the good, is always only direction. [Rogers: Uh huh] Not a substance.

103. ROGERS: Uh huh. Right. And if I get the the last portion of that particularly, you're saying that perhaps we can help the individual to strengthen the "yes," that is to affirm life rather than refuse it. Is that—

104. BUBER: M-hmmm. M-hmm. And, you see, I differ only in this word, I would not say "life." I would not put an object to it.

105. ROGERS: Uh huh.

106. BUBER: I would say simply "yes."

107. ROGERS: Uh huh. Uh huh. Uh huh. Uh huh. [4.0]

108. ROGERS: You're [to Friedman] looking as though you want to say something. [Unintelligible] Well, I could—

mentally a relational phenomenon, that what is "deepest" in the person—once barriers, psychological and social, could be surmounted—is a tendency toward relation. It was illuminating for Buber to elaborate on his nuanced understanding of polar reality. Yet in doing so, he overlooked something also subtle and inviting about what Rogers had actually said.

103–110. Transcription: (a) Previous transcripts inexplicably remove Rogers's comment "Right" in turn 103, obscuring the fact that Rogers in some way *agrees with* Buber's statement about polar reality, probably in particular that the good is a direction not a substance. ("The good life is a *process*, not a state of being. It is a direction, not a destination," Rogers observed in an essay written sometime in the late 1950s (Rogers, 1961, p. 186). The vocal inflection on Rogers's "right" suggests, to us at least, that he was agreeing, rather than simply encouraging Buber's further commentary. After the perception check, Buber then responds with vocalized pauses (one of which is omitted in the CR and P transcripts; both are omitted in the B-F transcript) that sound on tape also like agreement rather than mere acknowledgment. Buber differs

109. FRIEDMAN: I'm tempted to—

110. ROGERS: Well, we could, we could go on forever in the—

only in his minor objection to Rogers's use of the global term "life." After this interchange, the mood of the conversation seems conciliatory, as though each man might have been impressed by something in the other's positions. (b) The CR and P transcripts omit turns 105–107 and 109, and merge 108 and 110; the B-F transcript omits all of turns 105–110. The B-F deletion is interesting because in it Rogers is again fulfilling his facilitation role by recognizing verbally that the previous issue was in some sense closed, and they were ready for a transition. At this time, Friedman evidently signals nonverbally that he'd like to talk and Rogers recognizes him. When he doesn't respond immediately, it appears that Rogers starts to draw the evening to a close (he had asked his "one other question" after he noted that "time is going by" [turn 97]).

V

Acceptance and Confirmation

111. FRIEDMAN: My function as, as moderator, one, is to uh sharpen issues and I feel that there are two interrelated things that have been touched on here, but maybe not brought out, and I feel they're especially important, I'd like to to see. When, uh, when uh Dr. Rogers first asked uh Professor Buber about his attitude toward psychotherapy, he mentioned as one of the factors that enters into his [Buber: Hum] approach to therapy, "acceptance." Uh, now, Professor Buber, as we saw last night, often uses the term "confirmation," and it is my own feeling, from both what they said tonight and my knowledge of their writings, that it might be of real [Buber: Uh huh] importance to to clarify uh whether [Buber: Uh hum] they mean somewhat the same. [Buber: Hmmm] Um, Dr. Rogers writes uh about acceptance, uh in addition to saying that it's a rega-, a warm regard for the other and a respect for his individuality, for he's a person of

111. Transcription: (a) Previous transcripts change several readily understandable sentences to different understandable sentences. For one example among many, the phrase "that enters" has been transcribed as "which entered." (b) The B-F transcript omits Friedman's reference to Buber's presentation the previous evening. (c) The B-F transcript rearranges the words "Dr. Rogers writes" in the statement in order to signal more clearly where the quotation is about to begin. (d) For some reason, existing transcripts omit part of the quotation Friedman reads from Rogers's essay. The omitted portion, "how negative or positive, no matter . . . ," was also included in the essay when it was published (Rogers, 1961, p. 34), and it is hard to imagine why Rogers's transcriber (or Friedman) would consider it an insignificant portion of the quotation. (e) Friedman makes other minor changes in the quotation as he reads it orally.

unconditional worth, that it means "An acceptance of and regard for his attitudes of the moment, no matter how negative or positive, no matter how much they may contradict other attitudes he has held in the past," and "This acceptance of each fluctuating aspect of this other person makes it for him a relationship of warmth and safety."[23] Now, I wonder whether Professor Buber would look on confirmation as similar to that, or would he see confirmation as including, uh, perhaps not being accepted, including some demand on the other that that might mean in a sense a nonacceptance of his feelings at the moment in order to confirm him later.

Content/Process: (a) Rogers's observation that Friedman looked like he wanted to speak has given Friedman the floor to clarify an issue, consistent with how he described his role as moderator in introducing the dialogue. (b) Friedman appears to be framing his question in order to etch a distinction between Buber and Rogers more sharply. It sounds as if he is suggesting that agreement between self and other is a point of distinction between acceptance and confirmation, and that Rogers must believe that acceptance means agreement with the client's views of reality and self. Rogers does not, however, and Friedman's reading of Rogers's essay appears selective. Note that in using the phrase "nonacceptance of his feelings at the moment in order to confirm him later" to characterize Buber's position, Friedman shifts ground somewhat and overlooks that this is a different sense of "acceptance" than the one Rogers used. Rogers also in some ways struggled and disagreed with clients and did not automatically or simply agree with their often distorted perspectives, although he tried to accept those perspectives as real to the clients. But he claimed that this disagreement must be anchored in a basic

---

23. Friedman was quoting Rogers's then unpublished essay "Some Hypotheses Concerning the Facilitation of Personal Growth," which become chapter two of his *On Becoming a Person* (1961, p. 34).

respect for the other as a person. In the very paragraph following the one Friedman quoted, from his then unpublished essay (1961, p. 34), Rogers specifically refers to what must be accepted in the client as often so "horrible," "weak," "sentimental," or "bizarre" as to warrant disbelief; yet without these things being "accepted" as real to the client, and then understood, no progress toward the solution of client problems was possible. To Rogers, acceptance did not mean that Rogers-as-therapist fully believed in the veracity of a psychotic's view of reality, for instance, but that the therapist—by accepting the other's views as real and reasonable to the client, whether the therapist personally believes them or not—confirms for the client that he or she is important. That recognition helps to free the growth potential in the relationship. Although Rogers attempts to clarify all of this later in the dialogue, Buber is openly invited by Friedman's question to separate his concept from Rogers's. It is therefore difficult to see this as a clarification or a sharpening of the issues. (c) This was not the first time Friedman had asked Buber about this issue. Friedman first called Buber's attention to the relationship of confirmation and acceptance in a letter nearly a year earlier. Among the questions he and Leslie Farber suggested Buber might want to address during his seminars at the Washington School of Psychiatry, were "the problem of *confirmation* and its implications to psychotherapy," "the difference between true and false confirmation," and "Carl Rogers talks of 'complete acceptance' of the 'client' by the therapist. Is this ever possible? Is this always possible?" (Friedman, 1956b). It is reasonable to assume, therefore, that part of Buber's context for this evening's question was the assumption that Rogers advocated complete acceptance.

112. BUBER: Hmm. I would say [4.0] eh [5.1] every [2.9] true, let's say, existential relationship between two persons eh begins with acceptance. Acceptance—by "acceptance" *I* mean—perhaps eh the two eh concepts are eh not just alike—but by eh, eh "acceptance" I eh mean hmm [5.1] being able to eh tell, or to, rather not to tell, but only to make it felt to the other person, eh that I accept him just as he is. [Rogers: Uhm hum] Eh, I take you just as you are. Eh, well, so, but [2.6] it is not yet what I mean by "*confirm* the other." Because *accepting*, this is just eh accepting how the other is in this moment, in this eh actuality of his. Confirming means [4.5] first of all, eh, accepting the whole potentiality of the the other [Rogers: Uh huh] eh and making even a decisive difference in his potentiality, eh distinguishing between—and this is, of course, eh, eh [Buber

112. Transcription: (a) The B-F transcript deletes Buber's comment about the two concepts perhaps not being "just alike." It is not clear whether the "two concepts" phrase refers to "acceptance" and "confirmation" or to *his* view of acceptance contrasted with *Rogers's* view of acceptance. (b) Although Buber says "I can say it only in this form," existing transcripts substitute "word" for "form" (even though what follows is not a single word). (c) The CR and P transcripts introduce a significant error that Friedman corrects in B-F: They have Buber saying "being man to become," although that makes little sense. Actually, Buber referred to "being meant to become," a phrasing of Buber's concept of the unique calling that—when responded to—provides direction to a life. (d) Another serious error occurs two sentences later, where Buber has

sighs twice] we can eh be mistaken again and again in this, but it's just eh a chance between eh human beings. Eh, I can eh recognize in him, know in him, more or less, the person he has been—I can say it only in this form—*created* to become. Eh, in the simple factual language, eh we find not the terms for it because we don't find in it the term, the concept, "being meant to become." This is what we must, eh as far as we can, eh grasp, eh if not in the first moment, then after this. And now, I not only accept the other as he is, but I confirm him, in myself, and then in him, in relation to this potentiality that is *meant* by him and it can now be eh developed, it can evolve, it can enter eh a reality of life. He can eh do [3.3] more or less to this scope but I can, too, do something. And eh this is with with goals even deeper than acceptation. Eh, let's eh take, for example, eh man and a woman, man and wife. And eh he says, not expressly, but just by his whole relation to her, eh "I accept you as you are." But this does not mean, "I don't want you to change." But it eh says, "I discover in you, just by my accepting love, I eh discover in you what you are *meant* to become." Eh, this is, of course, not anything to be eh expressed in missive terms. [Rogers: Uh huh] But eh it may be that it eh grows and grows with the years of common life. [Rogers: Uh huh] [3.5]

been quoted as saying that a person's potentiality can "answer the reality of life." Although this call and response metaphor sounds elegant, it also is somewhat perplexing. What might Buber mean? He actually said that such potential "can enter eh a reality of life"—a much more accessible and sensical metaphor. (e) Finally, and also a significant mishearing, is the repetition in previous transcripts of Buber saying that confirmation is not expressed in "massive" terms. This strange and puzzling usage could suggest that Buber's command of the language was inadequate. To the contrary, however, Buber was quite precise. He said that the communication of confirmation was not expressed in *missive* terms—that is, confirmation is normally "expressed" implicitly as part of our behavior, and is not normally made explicit and coded in the verbal language. This is an elegant expression on Buber's part of what Bateson (1951) called the "command" function of language and Watzlawick, Beavin, and Jackson (1967) called the "relationship" level of communication. In addition, Buber's point that confirmation is "not anything to be eh expressed in missive terms" also plays on a religious connotation of missive as a communique that often represents authority and prescription; confirmation cannot be demanded.

Content/Process: (a) Buber explicitly defines acceptance by using the term itself; acceptance is "accepting" the momentary actuality of another. Yet confirmation to him is more. It includes accepting the "whole potentiality" of the other and even going further to make a "decisive difference" in that potentiality. Rogers clarifies in his next available turn after Friedman's question that he, too, believes that acceptance of potentiality is crucial, not just acceptance of the present self. This might have laid the disagreement to rest; the two are simply using different umbrella terms for the process. Rogers uses "acceptance" to include both accepting the other's present self and his or her potential, while Buber reserves "acceptance" to acknowledge who the other is now, but prefers "confirmation" to refer to the overall process that includes the possibility of affecting the potential of the other. Unfortunately, this semantic distinction was never clarified within the dialogue. (b) Buber's examples leave something to be desired. He seems to illustrate his disagreement through the "man and wife" example ("And eh he says, not expressly, but just by his whole relation to her. . . .") The analogy is odd on three counts. First, Buber actually says "accepting" here when the context would seem to suggest he meant "confirming." Second, Rogers has not said he wouldn't want his client to change—indeed, change is the basic purpose of psychotherapy—

so Buber's point cannot be taken to apply directly to what a Rogerian therapeutic position might be. Rogers found that when people are accepted as they are, then, paradoxically, they are able to change (e.g., in this dialogue, see turn 115 below—when "I am, exactly as I am, . . . fully accepted—then I can't help but change"). Third, it is odd that Buber did not state his position in more relational terms. Why, from his own dialogic perspective, should a psychotherapist assume that a husband (or any person, for that matter) knows what or who someone else is "meant to become"? (c) Rogers must have been impressed by Buber's use of confirmation, because he quotes Buber from this dialogue in "The Characteristics of a Helping Relationship," a significant essay he wrote shortly thereafter (see Rogers, 1961, p. 55), and occasionally in other places throughout his life (e.g., Rogers, 1980, p. 155).

113. ROGERS: Well, I think that um—

113. Transcription: This turn was deleted in previous transcripts.

114. BUBER: This is what you mean? [Rogers: Uh huh. Yes, yes.] Good.

114. Content/Process: Buber thoughtfully checks back with Rogers, perhaps adapting to Rogers's conversational style somewhat, and inviting his partner to elaborate.

115. ROGERS: And I think that sounds very much like the quality that uh [2.5] is in the experience that I think of as acceptance,

115. Content/Process: This is an exceptionally clear statement of Rogers's position on acceptance. He makes it clear that—as thera-

though I have tended to put it differently. I, I think that we do accept the individual *and* his potentiality. It's, I think it's a real question whether we could *accept* the individual as he is, because often he *is* in pretty sad shape perhaps [Buber: Uh hmm], if it were not for the fact we also—in some sense—realized and recognized his potentiality. I guess I feel, too, that, um, that acceptance of the most complete sort, acceptance of this person as he is, is the strongest factor making for change that I know. In other words, I think that does release change or release potentiality to find that as I *am*, exactly as I *am*, I am fully accepted—then I can't help but change. [3.9] Because then, I feel, there, then, [Rogers clears throat] then there is no longer any need for defensive barriers, so then what takes over are the forward moving processes of life itself, I think. [4.3]

pist—he does not often "accept" (in the restricted sense of agreeing with) clients' realities, even while he has to accept as real (in the sense of confirming) who the client is.

116. BUBER: I'm afraid I'm not so sure of that [Rogers: Uh huh] as you are, perhaps because I'm *not* a therapist. [Rogers: Hhm] And eh, eh I eh have necessarily to do eh with the problematic side in problematic man. [Rogers: Uh huh, uh huh] Eh, I *cannot* do—in my relationship to it, to him, my relationship to him—without just this. I cannot put this aside. I have just, as I said, I have to do with both men. I have to do with the problematic in him. And I have—eh,

116. Transcription: (a) Existing transcripts substitute "that problematic type" for what Buber actually said in the second sentence, "the problematic side in problematic man." This change appears to alter the meaning noticeably. Following the comment that Buber is not a therapist, "that problematic type" implies that he nevertheless has had significant experience with the kind of clients Rogers must see. However, it is more difficult to infer that mean-

eh—there *are* cases when I must help him *against* himself. He wants my help against himself. He wants, you see, he—the first thing of all is that he trusts me. Yes, life has become eh baseless for him. He cannot tread eh on firm eh soil, on firm earth. He is, so to say, suspended in the air. And, what does he want? What he wants is a being not only whom he has, he can trust as a man trusts another, but a being that gives him now the certitude "There *is* a soil. There *is* an existence. [Buber apparently hits the table on "is" in both of the previous two sentences] [Rogers: Uh huh] The world is *not* [Buber hits table] condemned [Rogers: Uh huh] eh to deprivation, degeneration, eh, destruction. [Rogers: Uh huh] Eh, the world *can* be redeemed. *I* can be redeemed *because there is this trust*" [Buber hits the table four times as he says "because there is this"] [Rogers: Uh huh]. And if this is eh reached, now I can help this man even in his struggle against himself. And this I can only do if I eh distinguish between "accepting" and "confirming."

ing from his *actual* words—which sound more like a general statement about his experience with what is problematic in humanity overall. (b) Most of the emphases on words and phrases in Buber's turn were not noted in previous transcripts, thereby sacrificing information about his intent. He also evidently hits the table several times, punctuating a particularly emphatic statement.

Content/Process: (a) Somewhat ironically, Buber thinks Rogers stated his position with sureness and certainty, while Buber is "not so sure of that"—"perhaps because I'm not a therapist." This provisionality from Buber contrasts sharply with his overall tone of certainty in the dialogue (see Cissna & Anderson, 1994, for a fuller analysis of this issue), yet he continues in this turn to state his position rather unequivocally and emphatically. Although the comment about him not being a therapist could be read as an ironic or even sarcastic comment on Rogers's opening question (Friedman [1994, p. 62] believes it was "unintentional irony"), sarcasm was not the tone we heard on the tape. On a related point, in the brief utterance that Buber interpreted as Rogers's certainty, Rogers consistently used such equivocal terms as "I think" (six times), "I guess I feel, too," and so forth. (b) As we noted before, Buber's statement, although framed as a disagreement with Rogers, does not seem essentially opposed to Rogers's ideas as developed in this dialogue or in his prior writing. Rogers also dealt with problematic persons, and helping them "against" the force of their own entrenched problems (as Buber might have put it) is a therapist's goal as well. It is a goal facilitated—as Rogers often said and wrote—by the very kind of relational trust Buber emphasizes. In his clinical case summaries, Rogers noted through similarly vivid metaphors that clients felt "baseless," as though they were "suspended in the air" without "firm earth" to trod (see especially similar metaphors from a client in an essay by Rogers ["What It Means to Become a Person"] that both Friedman and Buber had read and that both cite later in the dialogue [Rogers, 1961, pp. 120–121]). (c) When Buber finishes with "And this I can only do if I eh distinguish between 'accepting' and 'confirming,' it is in this context something of a *non sequitur*—because nowhere in his comments has he suggested why he must make this semantic distinction in order to help others. Yet this distinction has often been cited (Friedman, 1965, pp. 28–31; 1983, pp. 40–41; 1985, pp. 135–137; 1986; 1994, pp. 58–64; Kron & Friedman, 1994, pp. 80–82) as a major difference between Buber and Rogers.

117. ROGERS: I just feel that one um difficulty with a dialogue is that there could easily be no end,

117–121. Transcription: (a) The CR and P transcripts delete some words and substitute others in var-

but I think that uh both in mercy to Dr. Buber and to the audience, this is—so I will not—[Buber overlaps] [Laughter]

118. BUBER: This—what do you say?

119. ROGERS: I say that out of, out of consideration for you and consideration to—

120. BUBER: Not for me. Heh heh.

121. ROGERS: Oh, all right—[Laughter]—just just consideration for the audience—

ious places. (b) Heard on tape, this entire interchange is more light-hearted and friendly, with more laughter, than readers of previous transcripts might imagine. (c) The B-F transcript omits this entire interchange of five turns.

Content/Process: At this time, about 87 minutes had passed, although the audience had been told the event would last about an hour. Rogers may have felt the tension between his acknowledged facilitation role and a desire to reply to Buber's previous comment. If so, he opts for the former by appearing to introduce a transition to the event's conclusion. Turn 117 seems an implicit statement that he could reply, but will forego doing so because of the time constraints. Mentioning "mercy," however, perhaps implied to Buber that the older man's age or some other problem might have motivated Rogers's fairly abrupt transition; perhaps Buber heard this as a condescending comment. In any event, Buber wanted the group to know that he was willing to continue if Rogers was. No one can know precisely what motivated either man, but considering the pauses, hesitations, and restarts in recent turns, Buber did sound as though he was becoming tired, and Rogers's comment might have been justified in that sense.

VI

Within and Between

122. FRIEDMAN: May I be so unmerciful as to just ask one last question? And that is [Buber: Uh hum]: My um impression is that, on the one hand, there has been more insistence by Dr. Rogers on the full rec-, —full*er* reciprocity of the I-Thou relation in therapy and less by um Dr. Buber, but on the other, I get the impression that Dr. Rogers is more client-centered as the—

122. Transcription: (a) The B-F transcript deletes Friedman's reference to being "so unmerciful" in asking his last question, which recalled the mercy Rogers invoked in turn 117 in attempting to bring the dialogue to a close. (b) All previous transcripts delete evidence of Friedman correcting himself midway through the second sentence. He starts to say that Rogers insisted on the "full" reciprocity of therapist and client, but revises "full" to "fuller."

Content/Process: Although in mid-sentence Friedman changes "full" to "fuller," in recognition of the limits Rogers actually claimed, in subsequent commentaries Friedman has interpreted this issue very differently (cf. Friedman, 1983, pp. 225–226; 1986, pp. 409, 417–418; 1991, p. 368; 1992, pp. 41–56). For example, Friedman (1965) writes in the introductory essay to Buber's *The Knowledge of Man* in which he reprints the dialogue: "The issue between Martin Buber and Carl R. Rogers also concerns the therapist-patient relationship: Must it be based on a one-sided inclusion, as Buber holds, *or on full mutuality at every level, as Rogers claims?"* (p. 31, emphasis added). Not only is it clear from the tape of this dialogue that Rogers never argued for full mutuality (much less "full mutuality at every level"), but it is also clear from the tape that Friedman himself revised that characterization in midsentence while moderating the event.

123. BUBER: What?

123. Transcription: This turn is deleted in the B-F transcript.

124. FRIEDMAN: More client-centered—more concerned [Laughter]—more concerned, more concerned with the becoming of the, of the person. And he speaks in his second article[24] of, of being able to trust one's organism, that it will find, uh, satisfaction, that it will express *me*. And he speaks of the locus of value as being inside one, whereas I get the impression uh from my encounter with Dr. Buber that he sees value as more in "the between." I wonder, is this a real issue between the two of you? [5.7]

124. Transcription: (a) The B-F transcript streamlines this language somewhat, making it clearer and more readable. (b) The CR and P transcripts put no quotation marks around "the between." Friedman, in B-F, includes quotation marks because he recognizes this term as a discrete concept from Buber's work. (c) Previous transcripts do not include the long silence after Friedman's question; noting it here clarifies Rogers's next statement. On the tape it sounds as if Rogers was somewhat flustered at the beginning of turn 125, perhaps expecting Buber to address himself to the question first—and Rogers waited a long time (conversationally speaking)

---

24. Friedman was referring to the unpublished manuscript of Rogers's "What It Means to Become a Person," subsequently published as chapter six of *On Becoming a Person* (1961).

for Buber to speak if he should wish to do so.

Content/Process: Friedman cited this essay by Rogers ("his second article") as a contrast to Buber's thought about "the between." In it, Rogers attempted to describe the different feelings and attitudes experienced by clients who had been in therapy, and much of the essay presents direct quotations from them. He was not attempting to characterize the therapeutic relationship itself (a topic that presumably would have been closer in spirit to Buber's notion of "the between"), nor was he discussing theoretically what a therapist could do to facilitate that relationship. Therefore, this piece was hardly the best source for finding similarities. Rogers was writing about a different phenomenon.

125. ROGERS: [Buber: Hmm] I might just, um [2.5] give one type of expression to my view on that that, um, puts it in quite different terms than what you've used, and yet I think is is really relates to the same thing. That um [3.8] as I've tried to think about it in in recent months,[25] it seems to me that you uh could speak of the goal toward which therapy moves, and I guess the goal toward which maturity

125. Transcription: (a) Previous transcripts have changed a number of words early in this turn, to little effect. (b) In a significant change, the word "tonight" has been added in previous transcripts—beginning with the first CR transcript. Using "tonight" implies that Rogers referred to what was (or was not) shared *that night* between him and Buber. However, because he never said "tonight," we should recon-

---

25. We suspect Rogers was alluding to his work on two essays, "A Process Conception of Psychotherapy" and "'To Be That Self Which One Truly Is': A Therapist's View of Personal Goals." Both essays were presented at conferences in 1957, and they later became chapters seven and eight, respectively, of *On Becoming a Person* (1961).

moves in an individual, uh, as being "becoming," or, or, or being, being knowingly and acceptingly that which one most deeply *is*. In other words, that, that too expresses a real trust in the uh [2.9] process which we *are* that um perhaps may not entirely be shared between us.

sider his comment in light of two different possibilities. First, remember that Rogers was responding to a question about "the between." Syntactically, the statement as uttered sounds more like it references the relationship *between therapist and client*. To believe that Rogers referred to his relation to Buber would necessitate believing that the last sentence uses "we" and "us" to refer to different relationships. Still, it is mysterious why the word "tonight" would be added to a typescript that Rogers himself circulated, if he didn't think it somehow clarified his thought. One possibility is that Rogers didn't proofread the transcript—or didn't proofread it carefully—and simply overlooked this inappropriate insertion.[26] As a second interpretation, perhaps Rogers meant "we" to indicate the processual nature of persons (we human beings) and "us" to refer to himself and Buber. Rogers might have been indicating that he trusted that process of becoming while suggesting that Buber didn't trust it quite as much.

Content/Process: Rogers's statement is not very responsive to Friedman's question, except that it stresses the trust in growthful process that Rogers believes Buber does not share.

---

26. The Rev. Russell J. Becker, Ph.D., who studied with Rogers in the Counseling Center at the University of Chicago, said that he thought it unlikely that Rogers would have personally proofread the transcript because it would have been inconsistent with his typical work habits (personal communication, October 18, 1995).

126. BUBER: Now, eh [3.8 with sigh] perhaps it would be of a certain aid if I add [3.7 with sigh] a problem that that eh I found when reading just this article [Rogers: Uh huh] of yours, eh, or a problem that eh [Buber sighs] approached *me.* [Rogers: Uh huh] Eh, you speak about persons, and the concept "person" is eh seemingly um very near eh to the concept "individual." I would eh, eh think that it's advisable to distinguish between them. An individual is eh just eh, eh a certain uniqueness of a human eh being. And eh if it can, eh, eh, it can develop, eh, just by developing with uniqueness. Eh, this is what Jung calls "individuation." Eh, a pers-, that eh, eh—he may, he may become more and more and more an individual without making him more and more a *human.* [3.6] Eh, I have eh a [Rogers: Uh huh] lot of examples [Rogers: Uh huh] of man having become very, very individual, very distinct of others, very developed in their *such-and-suchness*, without eh eh being at all what I would like to call a man. [Rogers: Uh huh] Eh, therefore, *person*, I would sa-, individual is just this, this uniqueness, it can eh, being able to be developed, eh, eh, so and so. But person, I would say, is only an individual living really with the world. Not—and with the world, I don't mean *in* the world [Rogers: Uh huh], but just *in real contact*, in *real reciprocity* of the world in all the points in which the world

126–127. Transcription: (a) Buber did not say that it would perhaps aid the discussion if he could "ask a problem"; although that phrase appears in each previous transcript, it makes almost no sense. What he *did* say is quite clear and meaningful—he wants to "add" (to the conversation) a problem that he experienced when reading Rogers's article. (b) The B-F transcript makes several word substitutions that, while not inconsistent with Buber's original statements, do not add much either (e.g., "becoming" was substituted for "making him"; "know many" for "have a lot of," and "thus and thus" for "so and so"). (c) Previous transcripts fail to note that Rogers softly—but quite significantly—added "Correct" (turn 127) to Buber's comment about being against individuals, but for persons. This acknowledged point of agreement might surprise some of Rogers's critics, who accuse him of advocating a selfish individualism.

Content/Process: (a) Rogers probably thought Buber was "correct" because in many ways Buber simply summarized the theme of Rogers's piece, even though Buber sounded as though he was disagreeing by couching his observations as "a problem that that eh I found when reading just this article of yours." This is, at best, a puzzling statement perhaps made while Buber was tired or distracted; at worst, it is an unfair characterization of Rogers's posi-

can meet man. [2.7] Eh, I, I don't say only with man, because sometimes we meet the world in other shapes than in that of man. But this is what I would call a person, and, eh, I'm, eh if I may eh say expressly "yes" and "no" to certain phenomena, I'm *against* individuals and *for* persons.

127. ROGERS: Uhm huh. Correct. [Very quickly, very softly—not into microphone?] [4.6] [Applause]

tion in the article and elsewhere. Buber says Rogers uses the word "person" and that his concept of person is "seemingly um very near eh to the concept 'individual.'" He then proceeds to object to the word Rogers *didn't* use and that Buber himself introduced. Rogers actually explains in the essay that individuals are not necessarily "persons," but become so by their increasing ability to come into realistic contact with the world. Thus, it is surprising to hear Buber say "I would eh, eh think that it's advisable to distinguish between them" [individual and person], as though Rogers had taken a different position. An alternate interpretation is that Buber was trying to express—in a way he thought complimentary to Rogers—that he realized this problem or had his thinking about it clarified through reading Rogers's article. This interpretation, while generous, seems unlikely. Buber elsewhere in the dialogue was clear and direct when complimenting Rogers; why not here, if that was his intent? (b) Thorne (1992, pp. 69–75) reads this comment of Buber's as a wholesale assault on Rogerian theory. To Thorne, Buber implies that Rogers's therapy produces "individuals" (who are "very distinct" in their "such-and-suchness") rather than "persons" (who live in real reciprocity with the world). Although in some ways plausible, we also doubt this interpretation after hearing the tape, primarily because it presumes Buber's criticism to have been so indirect. Buber was willing earlier to be both forceful and clear in his criticisms of Rogers; we doubt he would resort here to such oblique strategies. (c) Two additional points help clarify these turns. First, the applause noted came after a pause, and did not seem to be in response to Buber or to Rogers but probably a reaction to a signal that the dialogue would end. Second, despite Rogers's verbalized assent at the end of Buber's comment, he didn't take this opportunity to expand his position, or, if Buber had misunderstood the article, to point that out. Perhaps he thought the timing was awkward, perhaps he reacted to the same nonverbal signal that triggered audience applause, or perhaps it was Rogers, acting within his role, who signaled the conclusion. For all practical purposes, then, the interchange between these two great thinkers ended unfortunately on a misunderstanding that would not have been recognized by listeners unfamiliar with Rogers's work.

Closing

128. FRIEDMAN: We have reason to be deeply indebted to Dr. Rogers and Dr. Buber for a, a unique dialogue. It is certainly unique in *my* experience: first, because it is a *real* dialogue, taking place in front of an audience, and and I think that, that is in part because of what they were willing to give us and did give us, and in part because you [the audience] took part, kind of a, in a trialogue, or adding me, a, a quatralogue in which you silently participated. [Applause—Buber says several unintelligible words during the applause]

128. Transcription: (a) The CR and P transcripts spell Friedman's word "triologue," but he changed that in the B-F transcript to "trialogue," a more euphonious analogue to "dialogue." (b) For some reason, the B-F transcript does not note audience applause after Friedman's conclusion.

Content/Process: (a) One reason this dialogue seemed unique to Friedman was that it occurred in front of an audience—thus creating conditions that Buber had previously predicted would deter dialogue. (b) Friedman's conclusion also underscores how even silence from an audience makes a positive contribution to genuine dialogue. In other studies (Anderson & Cissna, 1996b; Cissna & Anderson, 1994), we explore more specifically how an audience can function as a dialogic coauthor. (c) Although etymologically as well as in contemporary usage dialogue denotes "throughness" rather than "two-ness," several contemporary scholars have used such terms as "multilogue" and "polylogue" to refer to the special characteristics of multi-party dialogue. Perhaps Friedman used "trialogue" and "quatralogue" to suggest the distinctive types of participants in this event.

Conclusion

Central Contributions of a New Transcript

Despite the many tumultuous years that have passed since 1957, and despite the unpretentious and even innocent goals set for the Buber-Rogers meeting that April evening in Michigan, reconsidering their brief conversation becomes a curiously resonant experience for anyone concerned with the importance of authentic dialogue.

Scholars have long turned to the various transcripts of the Buber-Rogers dialogue for clues to these two similar approaches to human relationships—approaches that while complementary, nevertheless stress several different insights. Yet those same scholars, we have found, treat the text as thoroughly unproblematic, accepting one or another of the extant transcripts as given. Most scholars are evidently unaware of the rich history behind the conversation, and many seem unaware of, or unconcerned with, how the context, the different roles assigned to the principals, and their somewhat different interpersonal styles affected how the speakers reacted to each other. Yet the audiotape is clearly our best available text. We found three major reasons for returning to the spoken word, to produce a more accurate transcript with commentary.

The first contribution of a new transcript based on the recording is to reassert the important contributions both Buber and Rogers can make to contemporary cultural life (see Anderson & Cissna, 1996a). It would be fair to say that neither man is currently a superstar among academic theorists in the human studies, despite their obvious historical importance. The laudable ascendance of interdisciplinary cultural studies and critical theory makes celebrities of theorists who analyze power relations, cultural hegemonies, and the subtle strategies by which dominant groups advertise and impose their own interests while victimizing subordinate groups. To read how the philosopher and the psychotherapist conversed at midcentury seems almost quaint—even though their common concern turns out to be essentially the same relevant challenge that confronts postmodern theory: *how to turn toward, address, and respect otherness*. However, Bakhtin, Habermas, Lyotard, and Gadamer, among others, have emerged as somewhat trendier dialogic theorists than Buber, at least within what literary critics these days call theory. In addition, Rogers now is even occasionally denounced as simplistic or, worse, ignored in reviews of contemporary psychology, in spite of the odd irony that he is one of the most cited sources in American social science.

Against the backdrop of current debates about multiculturalism, uniqueness of identity, voices of power and victimage, communitarian responsibility, the postmodern contingency of meaning, and the competition among various theories of ideology, the lessons of Buber and Rogers may not leap to mind. They should. A focused, pointed lesson in intellectual history—perhaps like this one—could reconvene advocates of what Buber simply called "obedient listening" in dialogue (Friedman, 1991, p. 366). What Buber distilled in his philosophical anthropology, Rogers discovered through taking a somewhat different route; he attended carefully to his accumulating daily professional experience in the praxis of his clinical relations with clients. The convergence of the relatively discrete projects of Buber and Rogers may be the most remarkable meeting of philosophy and psychology in this century. Although Rogers was not interested in cloning himself as Buber's acolyte, and although some obvious differences distinguish their thought, each man's writing and teaching has introduced generations of teachers and scholars directly or indirectly to the work of the other scholar. Rogers both taught Buber to his students and cited Buber in his writing. The link is more indirect for Buber. *The Knowledge of Man*, which contains a transcript of the dialogue, is one of Buber's most popular books (Friedman, 1994, p. 47), and of course the prolific writing of Maurice Friedman has also functioned to introduce readers interested in Buber to the work of Rogers.

A second reason further justifies a new transcript. Any historical document important enough to be disseminated and reprinted this often (the original typescript has multiplied into three published versions and one substantive excerpt in English, and a German transcript as well) is important enough to be rendered accurately. Most recently, the 1989 volume *Carl Rogers: Dialogues* (Kirschenbaum & Henderson, 1989) and the 1988 reprint of Buber's 1965 book *The Knowledge of Man* with the dialogue appended (Buber, 1988) have brought the full dialogue back to scholarly attention, and—as we have shown—a variety of recent books and articles have referred prominently to it.

If errors in existing transcripts were trivial or sporadic, it would not be necessary or reasonable to publish a new version. On the contrary, quotation errors and other changes introduced in previous transcripts are surprisingly frequent and often thematically significant, even when Buber's and Rogers's basic positions seem clear enough. Stylistic editing, occasionally introduced with the expressed purpose of enhancing readability, has removed readers even further from what Buber and Rogers actually said, even when their speech on the tape made perfect sense. Both connotation and denotation have been affected, and some changes warped the contexts within which accurately transcribed utterances could be interpreted.

A fresh listen to the tape invites us to offer new information for students of social interaction and those interested in the relationship between Buber and Rogers. Although like previous transcribers we wanted to create a reader's transcript rather than a technically more accurate but less accessible document of conversational analysis, we chose to indicate many instances in which the conversants clearly stressed words and phrases that were not so noted previously (or clearly did not stress words and phrases that previous transcripts emphasized). We designate periods of silence as well as vocalized pauses that will be interesting for readers curious about Buber's and Rogers's states of mind, intentions, and perhaps even their feelings of weariness at the end of a long and difficult day. We include interjected comments, ranging from "Uh huh" and "Hmmm" to "Sure" and "Right," and also note when the principals have interrupted each other. Without this material (and little of it was represented accurately in previous transcripts), the relationship between Buber and Rogers in the dialogue simply cannot be well understood. They both agreed and disagreed, and told each other so. They accommodated each other's views—and even interaction styles—to some extent. They felt strongly about certain points and explained them more clearly than previous transcripts reported. They listened with extraordinary respect to each other, and each interrupted the other's speech to express things he thought important enough in this context to justify interrupting. Interaction newly noted in this transcript also clarifies the relationship between the stage group and an audience that probably understood it would not be able to question the speakers. Nevertheless, the audience felt comfortable enough to interact informally with the speakers several times during the dialogue.

The sheer quantity and centrality of changes introduced by previous transcribers should surprise Buber scholars, Rogers scholars, and others concerned with dialogic theory. A summary of especially significant changes might be helpful in establishing how problematic previous transcripts were, even if a reader has no immediate access to those other documents:

Turn 3: We have restored Rogers's references to the audience and to his difficulties arriving at the event. These comments establish a sense of immediacy with the audience, and set an informal tone that is maintained throughout.

Turn 4: A number of errors of fact and mishearing in previous reports of Buber's first substantive comment are corrected here.

Turn 4 and others: Previous transcripts failed to show how Rogers's silences and reluctance to interrupt his partner created conversational spaces that allowed for Buber's fuller elaboration of ideas. This was consistent with the stated role assignments: in some ways, the conversation took on the appearance and tone of an interview.

Turn 27: A phrase omitted from Rogers's question in other transcripts ("—or your experience—") is subtly important because it establishes what Rogers was actually requesting of Buber. He hoped that Buber would speak not just from his philosophy but—as Rogers himself planned to do—from his experience.

Turn 28: Buber's word "mode" (it seems unlikely he intended "mood," although his accent makes the word ambiguous) has been previously mistranscribed as "moment." This error is important because of the issue that later develops concerning whether mutuality is continuing and relatively full or just a matter of moments.

Turn 34: Buber says "he is, eh, from the moment he comes to you," rather than, as other transcripts have it, "he is floundering around, he comes to you." Buber is talking about a person, who, from the first, is entangled in the therapist's life. The person who needs help may be floundering, but Buber doesn't say that.

Turn 46: A significant initial mishearing of Buber's comment was actually reinforced by a phantom "but" edited into a subsequent transcript. Instead of saying "Yes. This is *not* what I mean" (CR transcript) or "Yes. *But* this is *not* what I mean" (B-F transcript), Buber actually said: "Yes. This is *just* what I mean" (emphases added).

Turn 50: Buber surely said that the *two* people, therapist and client, consider the client's experience, rather than that the therapist considers it "too." Although transcribing homophones (*two* and *too*) is always difficult, in this case, the context provides the clues that enable us to make a reasonable interpretation.

Turns 54–56: Many errors and changes in previous transcripts are corrected here. Most significantly, Buber does not say, "I'm not, so to say, 'Martin Buber' as, how do you say, with quotes"—although this exact assertion was attributed to him. In fact, "quotes" was one of a number of suggestions yelled from the audience, presumably to help Buber complete his meaning. He may have affirmed it nonverbally.

Turns 57–58: Rogers did not say "I realize that," as reported in other transcripts. Previous transcripts also omit Buber's turn without acknowledgment.

Turn 62: Buber has been misquoted several times in this utterance. For example, instead of "I must see you and him in this dialogue bounded by tragedy," he said that he saw therapist and client in dialogue "hampered by tragedy."

Turns 63–67: Buber had asked if Rogers had experience working with schizophrenics. Previous transcripts delete many of Rogers's assurances that he had dealt with them, even though schizophrenia was not the primary focus of his prior work. This point is important because some commentaries have emphasized that Buber was not surprised to hear that Rogers had *no* experience with schizophrenics. Previous transcripts also omit Buber's turn 70, a conversational acknowledgment of Rogers's experience with schizophrenics.

Turn 68: Some editing choices in previous transcripts reflect inferences about Buber's intentions. We have simply restored the original wording, to allow readers to judge for themselves.

Turns 75–79: We have corrected several inadequacies of previous transcripts, including noting interruptions in this interchange. We presume that scholars and other readers will be interested in the participants' attitudes toward each other, and (especially in a dialogue about dialogue) how they negotiate their own talk. Also, Buber said that what interests him "more than anything" is the "human eh effect of dialogue," rather than "human effective dialogue."

Turn 80: We corrected a transcriber's mishearing, "It's one thing to help the other," to what Buber actually said: "It's a question of wanting to help the other." More significantly, previous transcripts somewhat bewilderingly report that Buber identified a man in hell as a man in health; in fact, the word "health" is not uttered. Here and elsewhere, Buber was not particularly well served by the existing transcripts and editing. His speech was often more coherent and incisive than what was reported.

Turn 86: This is one of the most puzzling—and in some ways most significant—transcription errors in extant transcripts. Buber is quoted as saying "I'm with you," when he in fact says "Permission"; thus Buber here echoes and supports Rogers's usage, and demonstrates a listening style that is effective in showing his partner that he's been understood.

Turn 89: The most commonly cited transcript—from *The Knowledge of Man*—deletes an entire sentence and part of another from Rogers's turn: "Now I may be mistaken on that, I don't know. And what I mean by that is that. . . ." While the deletion is not crucial to the literal substance of his comment, it does demonstrate Rogers's well-known sense of provisionality in interviews, and his respect for the older scholar.

Turn 96: Buber's comment here—to the effect "modern psychology" does not sufficiently appreciate or utilize precise terminology—is (ironically) full of transcription errors and other alterations of its own terminology. To cite one representative example: Buber does not say "concepts are never reality," as he was quoted as saying; instead he appears to illustrate how body and soul—"physiologic" and "psychic"—are "mixed," with "consciousness a primal eh reality."

Turn 97: Many errors and adjustments also dot this turn of Rogers, including omitting his role-related recognition of how "time is going by." This is the kind of change that is perhaps of minimal value for readers focusing on the dialogue's philosophical content alone, but is significant for understanding how conversational process (how they talked) might have influenced content (what they talked about).

Turn 98: By removing Buber's comment from turn 98, the B-F transcript makes Rogers's question appear excessively long, repetitious, and somewhat inappropriate. In fact, Buber requested clarification and received it.

Turn 99: In addition to other changes, existing transcripts remove Rogers's comment acknowledging that his restatement is a "contrasting way" of putting the idea in question.

Turn 100: Among other errors in this turn, previous transcripts have Buber saying "unacceptable" although he says "inaccessible." That he does not say that problematic people are "unacceptable" is significant, first, because interpersonal accessibility is a rather different conceptual issue than acceptability, and second, because it changes the context for succeeding comments by both men.

Turn 102: A series of silences, one of almost nine seconds, is unnoted in previous transcripts. Although pauses are natural and pervasive features of conversation, extraordinary silences are significant in indicating those times when conversants are particularly thoughtful, hesitant, interested, or respectful. Silence and pauses—in this any many other turns—were a significant feature of this dialogue and were rarely noted in previous transcripts.

Turn 103: Rogers says "Right," at least partly agreeing with Buber's statement about the polar nature of reality. Some commentaries have suggested that Buber and Rogers were far apart on this issue, although the actual status of their disagreement may need to be reinterpreted in light of Rogers's previously unreported assent.

Turn 112: Several notable errors characterize this turn in previous transcripts. Most significantly, previous transcripts quoted Buber as claiming that confirmation in a marriage is not expressed in "massive" terms. This seems a puzzling and inappropriate adjective, until one listens to him on tape; he says that confirmation is not normally expressed in *missive* terms.

Turn 116: Extant transcripts fail to report Buber's quite understandable phrase "the problematic side in problematic man," and substitute "that problematic type." The connotation of the concocted statement is clearly different, seeming to imply that he has seen the kinds of clients Rogers sees as a therapist, although his actual utterance did not suggest this.

Turns 117–121: Readers of some earlier transcripts may have interpreted this interchange as confrontational, and the B-F transcript deletes it entirely. Heard on tape, this episode—along with the laughter it elicited—sounds quite friendly.

Turn 122: Other transcripts delete Friedman's self-correction of "full" to "fuller" while describing Rogers's view of the reciprocity of therapist and client, which affects the interpretation of Buber's and Rogers's views on mutuality or reciprocity in a therapeutic relationship.

Turn 125: Other transcripts report Rogers referring to a "real trust in the uh [2.9] process which we *are* that um may not entirely be shared between us tonight." This comment quite reasonably implies that he and Buber on that evening did not entirely share the same view of that kind of trust. However, *Rogers did not say "tonight"* at the end of his sentence. He may not have been referring to that evening's relationship between himself and Buber, but—given the context of previous statements—could have been referring to his relationship with any given client.

Turn 127: Rogers softly replies "Correct" when Buber says he's for persons, but against individuals, although no previous transcript reported this. This agreement is interesting not only because Buber seemed to frame his comment as a disagreement with Rogers's article (despite Buber essentially echoing the article's main theme), but because this idea is so removed from the selfish individualism that some critics assume Rogers advocates.

A final reason why a new transcript seems important is that it illuminates a critical incident in the careers of two of the most seminal thinkers in the 20th century's quest to explain human nature and experience. Although neither man later would cite this evening as pivotal in any specific or persistent way, we have isolated interesting evidence that points to its influence as a turning point for them both.

Although Rogers discovered that his intellectual affinity for Buber's ideas was not entirely reciprocated, he cited Buber's thought much more often after 1957, after the dialogue, and broadened his praxis to a somewhat more philosophical approach to communication and social responsibility (Cissna & Anderson, 1990). Van Balen identified two periods in Rogers's development, with 1957 being the dividing point. In 1957, two important events occurred: In addition to his April dialogue with Buber, that fall Rogers moved to Wisconsin where his work focused on schizophrenics.[27] Van Balen's conclusion was that the Buber-Rogers dialogue had a "crucial" impact on the evolution of Rogers's thinking (p. 66). In addition, in an article published seventeen years after the dialogue, Rogers himself describes the impact of his dialogue with Buber:

> *This recognition of the significance of what Buber terms the I-thou relationship is the reason why*, in client-centered therapy, there has come to be a greater use of the self of the therapist, of the therapist's feelings, a greater stress on genuineness, but all of this without imposing the views, values, or interpretations of the therapist on the client. (1974, p. 11; emphasis added)

On the evidence of this single dialogue, Buber explicitly changed his previous strong conviction that it is impossible to conduct genuine dialogue in front of an audience, or when the interaction is taped or filmed (see Friedman, 1983, p. 227). Although it is impossible to know how important Buber considered this concession to be at the time, its importance seems to loom very large in the context of contemporary debates about media, democratic discourse, and the viability of dialogue in the public sphere—all questions addressed more recently by a variety of cultural critics.

Buber's new postscript to *I and Thou* (Buber, 1958), written only months after the dialogue, also developed in more detail a view of psychotherapy (pp. 132–133) that was strikingly similar to that of Rogers—despite what Buber apparently thought was their differing definitions of mutuality, confirmation, and inclusion. In the postscript he criticizes any therapist who is content to "analyze" a "patient" (his terms). Instead, the "regeneration of an atrophied personal centre" (p. 133) can only be accomplished with a therapist who has "the person-to-person attitude of a partner, not by the consideration and examination of an object" (p. 133). Despite some differences of terminology, this was the essence of Rogers's own therapy, as described in the dialogue and shown

---

27. Van Balen identifies the publication of Rogers's famous article on the "Necessary and Sufficient Conditions of Therapeutic Personality Change" (1957b) as the other crucial event of that year in Rogers's life (in addition to the dialogue with Buber). In our view, however, its publication represents the culmination of Rogers's thinking over a period of time, and although it was a very important article, its publication was not itself an influential event in Rogers's life. The second crucial and formative event of that year, we believe, was Rogers's move from the University of Chicago Counseling Center to the University of Wisconsin to study and to engage in psychotherapy with schizophrenics.

by the impending publication of *On Becoming a Person* (1961), which contained several essays that Buber read in preparation for their 1957 dialogue. If Buber and Friedman thought Rogers understood Buber's philosophy only fragmentarily, they would have been hard pressed to identify an American therapist whose practice at that time enacted it more thoroughly. Rogers became more and more a therapist with the attitude of a partner, disaffiliating himself increasingly from what he saw as the objectifications of behavioral/Skinnerian and psychoanalytic/Freudian psychologies. In addition, Buber's description in his postscript of the limits to mutuality in a therapeutic relationship ("But again the specific 'healing' relation would come to an end the moment the patient thought of, and succeeded in, practising 'inclusion' and experiencing the event from the doctor's pole as well" [1958, p. 133]) seemed to echo Rogers in the dialogue ("If this client comes to the point where he can experience what he is expressing, but also can experience my understanding of it and reaction to it, and so on, then really therapy is just about over" [turn 45]). It might also be worth noting that Rogers echoed Buber's postscript in the years following their meeting: A decade later, Rogers cooperated with Barry Stevens in a book (1967) titled *Person to Person*, the very phrase approvingly previewed by Buber's discussion of psychotherapists a decade earlier in the newer edition of *I and Thou*. Some years after that work, Rogers used the "partners" motif as well in a book title (1972), though in a different context.

After the dialogue, Buber remarked that he admired how honestly and directly Rogers had approached the conversation (Friedman, 1957; 1983, p. 227; 1991, p. 370). He also noted to Friedman that he was kind to Rogers in that he could have been "much sharper" with him, but had held back (Friedman, 1983, p. 227).[28] Rogers, from his perspective, was convinced that the dialogue with the much-admired senior scholar was productive—with the single reservation, evidently, that he did not appreciate the need for a moderator (Friedman), if Rogers's own role was to be a questioner for Buber (see Friedman's opening turn). Consequently, because of the interplay of these two limitations (Buber evidently holding back critical comments and Rogers holding back from developing his ideas because of his interviewerlike role and the presence of another "interviewer"), the dialogue might not be a wholly exemplary model for intellectual discourse. Yet the two men confronted

---

28. In our interview with him, Seymour Cain reported that in his brief meeting with Buber immediately after the dialogue, Buber said that he treated Rogers "gently—like a boy" (August 10, 1993).

many central issues in 20th—and 21st—century life, confronted them with directness and immediacy, and confronted them in ways that were unique when compared with their previous writings.

Our culture has too few exemplars of public intellectuals actually learning something in public from each other. This is one. If a basic criterion of genuine dialogue is a productive immediacy, this was dialogue of a very high quality indeed. It was one of the most significant events of our recent intellectual history in the human studies. It deserves not only close attention but an accurate rendering.

References

Anderson, R. (1982). Phenomenological dialogue, humanistic psychology and pseudo-walls: A response and extension. *Western Journal of Speech Communication, 46,* 344–357.

Anderson, R., & Cissna, K. N. (1991). *The Buber-Rogers dialogue: Studying the influence of role, audience, and style.* A paper presented at the international interdisciplinary conference, "Martin Buber: His Impact on the Human Sciences," San Diego State University, San Diego.

Anderson, R., & Cissna, K. N. (1996a). *Buber, Rogers, and the theory of human relationships.* Paper presented at the Southern States Communication Association convention, Memphis.

Anderson, R., & Cissna, K. N. (1996b). Criticism and conversational texts: Rhetorical bases of role, audience, and style in the Buber-Rogers dialogue. *Human Studies, 19,* 85–118.

Arnett, R. C. (1981). Toward a phenomenological dialogue. *Western Journal of Speech Communication, 45,* 201–212.

Arnett, R. C. (1982). Rogers and Buber: Similarities, yet fundamental differences. *Western Journal of Speech Communication, 46,* 358–372.

Arnett, R. C. (1986). *Communication and community: Implications of Martin Buber's dialogue.* Carbondale: Southern Illinois University Press.

Arnett, R. C. (1989). What is dialogic communication?: Friedman's contribution and clarification. *Person-Centered Review, 4,* 42–60.

Attendence [*sic*] at the Martin Buber Conference. (1957). Michigan Historical Collections, Bentley Historical Library, University of Michigan.

Baldwin, D. (1957a). Baldwin to Buber, 11 January 1957, Jerusalem. Unpublished letter from the Martin Buber Archives, Jewish National & University Library, Arc. Ms. Var. 350/836d:2.

Baldwin, D. (1957b). Baldwin to Buber, 11 February 1957, Jerusalem. Unpublished letter from the Martin Buber Archives, Jewish National & University Library, Arc. Ms. Var. 350/836d:5.

Baldwin, D. (1957c). Baldwin to Buber, 8 April 1957, Washington, DC. Unpublished letter from the Martin Buber Archives, Arc. Ms. Var., Jewish National & University Library, 350/836d:8.

Baldwin, D. (1957d). Baldwin to Rogers, 8 April 1957, Chicago. Unpublished letter from The Carl R. Rogers Collection, Collections of the Manuscript Division, Library of Congress, Washington, DC (box 80, folder 13).

Bateson, G. (1951). Information and codification: A philosophical approach. In J. Ruesch & G. Bateson, *Communication: The social matrix of psychiatry* (pp. 21–49). New York: W. W. Norton & Company.

Brace, K. (1992). I and Thou in interpersonal psychotherapy. *The Humanistic Psychologist, 20*, 41–57.

Brink, D. D. (1987). The issues of equality and control in the client- or person-centered approach. *Journal of Humanistic Psychology, 27*, 27–37.

Buber, M. (1952a). Buber to Bedford, 26 December 1952. Unpublished letter from the Martin Buber Archives, Arc. Ms. Var., Jewish National & University Library, 217a/330.

Buber, M. (1952b). Buber to Friedman, 23 December 1952. Unpublished letter from the Martin Buber Archives, Arc. Ms. Var., Jewish National & University Library, 217a/327.

Buber, M. (1952c). Buber to Friedman, 31 December 1952. Unpublished letter from the Martin Buber Archives, Arc. Ms. Var., Jewish National & University Library, 217a/331.

Buber, M. (1957a). Elements of the interhuman. *Psychiatry, 20*, 105–113.

Buber, M. (1957b, April 17). Elements of the inter-human (R. G. Smith, Trans.). Paper presented at the Mid-West Conference with Dr. Martin Buber, Ann Arbor, MI.

Buber, M. (1957c). *Pointing the way: Collected essays* (M. Friedman, Trans. & Ed.). New York: Harper & Row.

Buber, M. (1958). *I and thou* (2nd ed.) (R. G. Smith, Trans.). New York: Charles Scribner's Sons.

Buber, M. (1965a). *Between man and man* (R. G. Smith, Trans.; M. Friedman, Intro.). New York: Macmillan.

Buber, M. (1965b). *The knowledge of man: A philosophy of the interhuman* (M. Friedman, Ed. & Intro.). New York: Harper & Row.

Buber, M. (1967). Replies to my critics. In P. A. Schilpp & M. Friedman (Eds.), *The philosophy of Martin Buber* (pp. 689–744). LaSalle, IL: Open Court.

Buber, M. (1973). *Meetings*. LaSalle, IL: Open Court.

Buber, M. (1988). *The knowledge of man: A philosophy of the inter-human* (M. Friedman, Ed. & Intro.; M. Friedman & R. G. Smith, Trans.; A. Udoff, New Intro.). Atlantic Highlands, NJ: Humanities Press International.

Buber, M. (1991). Buber to Leslie H. Farber, 19 February 1957, Jerusalem. In N. N. Glatzer & P. Mendes-Flohr (Eds.), *The letters of Martin Buber: A life of dialogue* (No. 665). New York: Schocken Books.

Burstow, B. (1987). Humanistic psychotherapy and the issue of equality. *Journal of Humanistic Psychology, 27*, 9–25.

Carl Rogers: Giving people permission to be themselves (1977, October 7). *Science, 198*, 1–33.

Cissna, K. N., & Anderson, R. (1990). The contributions of Carl Rogers to a philosophical praxis of dialogue. *Western Journal of Speech Communication, 54*, 125–147.

Cissna, K. N., & Anderson, R. (1994). The 1957 Martin Buber-Carl Rogers dialogue, as dialogue. *Journal of Humanistic Psychology, 34*, 11–45.

Cissna, K. N., & Anderson, R. (1996). Dialogue in public: Looking critically at the Buber-Rogers dialogue. In M. Friedman (Ed.), *Martin Buber and the human sciences* (pp. 191–206). Albany, NY: State University of New York Press.

Dialog zwischen Martin Buber und Carl Rogers (1992). *Integrative Therapie, 18*, 245–260.

Dialogue between Martin Buber and Carl Rogers (nd). Unpublished typescript, The Carl R. Rogers Collection, Collections of the Manuscript Division, Library of Congress, Washington, DC (box 80, folder 13), and the Carl Rogers Memorial Library, Center for Studies of the Person, La Jolla, CA.

Dialogue between Martin Buber and Carl Rogers (1957–1960). Unpublished mimeograph copy, The Carl R. Rogers Collection, Collections of the Manuscript Division, Library of Congress, Washington, DC (box 46, folder 6). (originally labeled "For Private Circulation Only—Not to be Published")

Dialogue between Martin Buber and Carl Rogers (1960). *Psychologia, 3*, 208–221.

Edwards, P. (1970). *Buber and Buberism: A critical evaluation*. Lawrence, KS: Department of Philosophy, University of Kansas.

Evans, R. I. (1975). *Carl Rogers: The man and his ideas*. New York: E. P. Dutton.

Farber, L. H. (1991). Farber to Buber, 9 April 1956, Washington, DC. In N. N. Glatzer & P. Mendes-Flohr (Eds.), *The letters of Martin Buber: A life of dialogue* (No. 656). New York: Schocken Books.

Friedman, M. (1952). Friedman to Buber, 23 December 1952. Unpublished letter from the Martin Buber Archives, Arc. Ms. Var., Jewish National & University Library, 217a/61.

Friedman, M. (1953). Friedman to Buber, 11 January 1953. Unpublished letter from the Martin Buber Archives, Arc. Ms. Var., Jewish National & University Library, 217a/63.

Friedman, M. (1955a). Friedman to Buber, 4 July 1955. Unpublished letter from the Martin Buber Archives, Arc. Ms. Var., Jewish National & University Library, 217a/101.

Friedman, M. S. (1955b). *Martin Buber: The life of dialogue*. Chicago: University of Chicago Press.

Friedman, M. (1956). Friedman to Buber, 27 July 1956. Unpublished letter from the Martin Buber Archives, Arc. Ms. Var., Jewish National & University Library, 217a/126.

Friedman, M. (1957). Friedman to Rogers, 23 April 1957, New York. Unpublished letter from The Carl R. Rogers Collection, Collections of the Manuscript Division, Library of Congress, Washington, DC (box 6, folder 1).

Friedman, M. (1964). Dialogue between Martin Buber and Carl Rogers. In M. Friedman (Ed.), *The worlds of existentialism: A critical reader* (pp. 485–497). New York: Random House.

Friedman, M. (1965). Introductory essay. In M. Buber, *The knowledge of man: A philosophy of the interhuman* (pp. 11–58). (M. Friedman, Ed. & Intro.). New York: Harper & Row.

Friedman, M. (1981). *Martin Buber's life and work: The early years—1878–1923*. New York: E. P. Dutton.

Friedman, M. (1983). *Martin Buber's life and work: The later years—1945–1965*. New York: E. P. Dutton.

Friedman, M. (1985). *The healing dialogue in psychotherapy*. New York: Jason Aronson.

Friedman, M. (1986). Carl Rogers and Martin Buber: Self-actualization and dialogue. *Person-Centered Review, 1*, 409–435.

Friedman, M. (1987). Reminiscences of Carl Rogers. *Person-Centered Review, 2*, 392–395.

Friedman, M. (1991). *Encounter on the narrow ridge: A life of Martin Buber*. New York: Paragon House.

Friedman, M. (1992). *Dialogue and the human image: Beyond humanistic psychology*. Newbury Park: SAGE Publications.

Friedman, M. (1994). Reflections on the Buber-Rogers dialogue. *Journal of Humanistic Psychology, 34*, 46–65.

Hycner, R. (1991). *Between person and person: Toward a dialogical psychotherapy*. Highland, NY: The Gestalt Journal.

Kelb, B. J. (1991). *Martin Buber's philosophy of dialogue and three modern rhetorics*. Doctoral dissertation, Purdue University.

Kirschenbaum, H. (1979). *On becoming Carl Rogers*. New York: Delacorte Press.

Kirschenbaum, H. (1995). Author's note. In M. M. Suhd, *Positive regard: Carl Rogers and other notables he influenced* (pp. 93–102). Palo Alto, CA: Science & Behavior Books.

Kirschenbaum, H., & Henderson, V. L. (Eds.). (1989). *Carl Rogers: Dialogues—Conversations with Martin Buber, Paul Tillich, B. F. Skinner, Gregory Bateson, Michael Polanyi, Rollo May, and others.* Boston: Houghton Mifflin.

Kron, T., & Friedman, M. S. (1994). Problems of confirmation in psychotherapy. *Journal of Humanistic Psychology, 34,* 66–83.

McLaughlin, M. L. (1984). *Conversation: How talk is organized*. Beverly Hills, CA: SAGE Publications.

Nofsinger, R. E. (1991). *Everyday conversation*. Newbury Park, CA: SAGE Publications.

Pentony, P. (1987). Some thoughts about Carl Rogers. *Person-Centered Review, 2,* 419–421.

Peterson, J. D. (1976). *Carl Rogers and his ways of being in interpersonal relationships*. Master's thesis, Kansas School of Religion and University of Kansas.

Program: Mid-West Conference with Dr. Martin Buber. (1957). Michigan Historical Collections, Bentley Historical Library, University of Michigan.

Rasmussen, R. Z. (1991). *Person-centered and dialogical counseling: A comparative study*. Doctoral dissertation, University of North Dakota.

Rendahl, S. E. (1975). *Carl Rogers and Martin Buber: A comparison of communication perspectives*. Doctoral dissertation, University of Minnesota.

Rieber, R. W. (1989). In search of the impertinent question: An overview of Bateson's theory of communication. In R. W. Rieber (Ed.), *The individual, communication, and society: Essays in memory of Gregory Bateson*. New York: Cambridge University Press.

Roffey, J. W. (1980). *A hermeneutic critique of counseling psychology: Ricoeur and Rogers*. Doctoral dissertation, University of Kentucky.

Rogers, C. R. (nd-a). Buber-79. Unpublished notes from the Carl R. Rogers Collection, Collections of the Manuscript Division, Library of Congress, Washington, DC (box 80, folder 13).

Rogers, C. R. (nd-b). Buber dialogue: Notes from tape. Unpublished notes from The Carl R. Rogers Collection, Collections of the

Manuscript Division, Library of Congress, Washington, DC (box 80, folder 13).

Rogers, C. R. (nd-c). Buber—Distance & relation. Unpublished notes quoting Buber from The Carl R. Rogers Collection, Collections of the Manuscript Division, Library of Congress, Washington, DC (box 82, folder 15).

Rogers, C. R. (nd-d). Buber's concept of inclusion. Unpublished handout (includes quotes from the "Education" chapter of Buber's *Between man and man*) from The Carl R. Rogers Collection, Collections of the Manuscript Division, Library of Congress, Washington, DC (box 140, folder 8).

Rogers, C. R. (nd-e). The life of dialogue. Unpublished notes (from M. S. Friedman's, *Martin Buber: The life of dialogue* [pp. 85–89]) from The Carl R. Rogers Collection, Collections of the Manuscript Division, Library of Congress, Washington, DC (box 80, folder 13).

Rogers, C. R. (nd-f). Martin Buber—*I & Thou* (Trans. by R. G. Smith, Edinburgh: T. & T. Clark, 1937): CR's summary. Unpublished notes from The Carl R. Rogers Collection, Collections of the Manuscript Division, Library of Congress, Washington, DC (box 113, folder 9).

Rogers, C. R. (nd-g). Martin Buber—*I & Thou* (Trans. by R. G. Smith, Edinburgh: Clark, 1950). Unpublished notes from The Carl R. Rogers Collection, Collections of the Manuscript Division, Library of Congress, Washington, DC (box 80, folder 13).

Rogers, C. R. (1942a). *Counseling and psychotherapy: New concepts in practice*. Boston: Houghton Mifflin.

Rogers, C. R. (1942b). The use of electrically recorded interviews in improving psychotherapeutic techniques. *American Journal of Orthopsychiatry, 12*, 429–434.

Rogers, C. R. (1951). *Client-centered therapy: Its current practice, implications, and theory*. Boston: Houghton Mifflin.

Rogers, C. R. (1956a, October 20). *The essence of psychotherapy: A client-centered view*. Paper presented at the first meeting of the American Academy of Psychotherapists, New York. From The Carl R. Rogers Collection, Collections of the Manuscript Division, Library of Congress, Washington, DC (box 126, folder 2). (Included in *Counseling Center Discussion Papers, 2*(26), 1956, University of Chicago.)

Rogers, C. R. (1956b, October 20). *The essence of psychotherapy: Moments of movement*. Draft of a paper presented at the first meeting of the American Academy of Psychotherapists, New

York. From The Carl Rogers Memorial Library, Center for Studies of the Person, La Jolla, CA.

Rogers, C. R. (1957a). Dialogue with Martin Buber: Nature of man as revealed in interpersonal rel. Unpublished notes from The Carl R. Rogers Collection, Collections of the Manuscript Division, Library of Congress, Washington, DC (box 46, folder 6).

Rogers, C. R. (1957b). The necessary and sufficient conditions of therapeutic personality change. *Journal of Consulting Psychology, 21,* 95–103.

Rogers, C. R. (1958a). Rogers to Buber, 23 January 1958, Jerusalem. Unpublished letter from Martin Buber Archives, Jewish National & University Library, Arc. Ms. Var. 350/622b:2.

Rogers, C. R. (1958b, February 20–21). A theory of psychotherapy with schizophrenics and a proposal for its empirical investigation. Paper presented at a symposium on "Psychotherapy with Schizophrenics," Southeast Louisiana State Hospital, Manderville, Louisiana. From The Carl R. Rogers Collection, Collections of the Manuscript Division, Library of Congress, Washington, DC (box 80, folder 15).

Rogers, C. R. (1959a). The essence of psychotherapy: A client-centered view. *Annals of Psychotherapy, 1,* 51–57.

Rogers, C. R. (1959b). Rogers to Oliver H. Bown, 14 July 1959, Madison, Wisconsin. Unpublished letter from The Carl R. Rogers Collection, Collections of the Manuscript Division, Library of Congress, Washington, DC (box 32, folder 5).

Rogers, C. R. (1960). Significant trends in the client-centered orientation. In L. E. Abt & B. F. Riess (Eds.), *Progress in clinical psychology* (Vol. 4; pp. 85–99). New York: Grune & Stratton.

Rogers, C. R. (1961). *On becoming a person.* Boston: Houghton Mifflin.

Rogers, C. R. (1966). Client-centered therapy. In S. Arieti (Ed.), *American Handbook of Psychiatry* (Vol. 3) (pp. 183–200). New York: Basic Books.

Rogers, C. R. (Ed.) (1967). *The therapeutic relationship and its impact: A study of psychotherapy with schizophrenics.* Madison: University of Wisconsin Press.

Rogers, C. R. (1969). *Freedom to learn.* Columbus, OH: Charles E. Merrill Publishing Co.

Rogers, C. R. (1972). *Becoming partners: Marriage and its alternatives.* New York: Dell Publishing Company.

Rogers, C. R. (1974). Remarks on the future of client-centered therapy. In D. A. Wexler & L. N. Rice (Eds.), *Innovations in client-centered therapy* (pp. 7–13). New York: John Wiley & Sons.

Rogers, C. R. (1977). Rogers to Tom Brouillette, 17 May 1977, La Jolla. Unpublished letter from The Carl R. Rogers Collection, Collections of the Manuscript Division, Library of Congress, Washington, DC (box 16, folder 3).

Rogers, C. R. (1980). *A way of being*. Boston: Houghton Mifflin.

Rogers, C. R. (1987). Comments on the issue of equality in psychotherapy. *Journal of Humanistic Psychology, 27*, 38–40.

Rogers, C. R., & Farson, R. E. (1957). *Active listening*. Chicago: Industrial Relations Center, University of Chicago.

Rogers, C. R., with Russell, D. E. (1991). *The quiet revolutionary* (Draft 1/25/91). Santa Barbara, CA: Library Oral History Program, University of California at Santa Barbara.

Rogers, C. R., & Stevens, B. (1967). *Person to person: The problem of being human—A new trend in psychology*. Lafayette, CA: Real People Press.

Sato, K. (1960). [Editor's note]. *Psychologia, 3*, no page number [immediately precedes p. 197].

Schaeder, G. (1973). *The Hebrew humanism of Martin Buber* (N. J. Jacobs, Trans.). Detroit: Wayne State University Press.

Seckinger, D. S. (1976). The Buber–Rogers dialogue: Theory confirmed in experience. *Journal of Thought, 11*, 143–149.

Streiker, L. (1969). *The promise of Buber: Desultory phillippics and irenic affirmations*. Philadelphia: J. P. Lippincott.

Tentative Program: Mid-West Conference on the Visit of Dr. Buber of Jerusalem to the University of Michigan. (1957). Unpublished document from The Carl R. Rogers Collection, Collections of the Manuscript Division, Library of Congress, Washington, DC (box 80, folder 13).

Thorne, B. (1992). *Carl Rogers*. London: SAGE Publications.

Upshaw, H. T. (1970). *The interdependence of the religious and the psychological considered through a comparison of the views of Martin Buber and Carl Rogers on the nature of personal meaning*. Doctoral dissertation, University of Chicago.

Van Balen, R. (1990). The therapeutic relationship according to Carl Rogers: Only a climate? A dialogue? Or both? In G. Lietaer, J. Rombauts, & R. Van Balen (Eds.), *Client-centered and experiential psychotherapy in the nineties* (pp. 65–85). Leuven: Leuven University Press.

Van Belle, H. A. (1980). *Basic intent and therapeutic approach to Carl R. Rogers: A study of his view of man in relation to his view of therapy, personality and interpersonal relations*. Toronto: Wedge Publishing.

Watzlawick, P., Jackson, D. D., & Beavin, J. H. (1967). *Pragmatics of human communication: A study of interaction patterns, pathologies, and paradoxes.* New York: W. W. Norton & Company.

Yocum, K. L. (1980). *Martin Buber's relational philosophy: The development of influence on communication education and humanistic education.* Doctoral dissertation, Ohio State University.

Yoshida, A. (1994). Beyond the alternative of "compulsion" or "freedom": Reflections on the Buber-Rogers dialogue. In D. M. Bethel (Ed.), *Compulsory schooling and human learning: The moral failure of public education in America and Japan* (pp. 89–102). San Francisco: Caddo Gap Press.

About the Authors

Rob Anderson, Professor and Director of Graduate Studies in the Department of Communication at Saint Louis University, is author, coauthor, or coeditor of six previous books in communication theory and practice, including *Students as Real People, Before the Story, Questions of Communication,* and *The Conversation of Journalism.* He makes his intellectual home at the junctions of interpersonal and mass media scholarship. His articles have appeared in various journals in the fields of speech communication, journalism, English, psychology, and education.

Kenneth N. Cissna is Professor of Communication at the University of South Florida. His articles have appeared in a variety of journals in communication and related fields, including *Communication Monographs, Communication Education, Western Journal of Speech Communication, Southern Speech Communication Journal, Small Group Behavior, Journal of Humanistic Psychology,* and *Human Studies,* as well as in several edited books. His most recent edited book, *Applied Communication in the 21st Century,* is an award-winning examination of theoretical, research, and pedagogical issues in applied communication.

The authors have published and presented numerous papers on dialogic communication and have coedited, with Ronald C. Arnett, *The Reach of Dialogue.* Their work on the Buber-Rogers dialogue over the last decade is summarized in this volume as well as in a forthcoming book from SUNY Press, *Martin Buber, Carl Rogers, and the Potential for Public Dialogue.*

Author Index

Subject Index